The New York Times

PRACTICAL BRIDGE

By Alan Truscott

with a Foreword by Omar Sharif

 GOLDEN PRESS · NEW YORK

Contents

Foreword

EVERYONE thinks there is no finer life than that of a movie star. Yet, if I had complete freedom to spend my time as I see fit, I would choose to play bridge most of my waking hours!

There is nothing quite like bridge. It is an intellectual challenge and a game of tactics, strategy, bluff, and applied psychology. And a marvelous outlet: where else can one unleash hostility and give free rein to the killer instinct without fear of maiming anyone?

Bridge is an elegant diversion. All daily cares are shed when you wrestle with a difficult hand and try to puzzle out which of your inscrutable opponents holds the vital queen of diamonds.

Yes, I have the greatest sympathy for anyone who has never been exposed to bridge, for he is denied an incomparable pleasure.

Alas, I cannot spend my whole life at the bridge table. But now that I have my own touring team of international stars—the Omar Sharif Bridge Circus—we play matches against the strongest teams we can find in Europe and America whenever I can escape from the world of movie studios and locations.

Benito Garozzo and Giorgio Belladonna of Italy—World Champions many times over—are on the team.

In one of our early matches, we recruited Alan Truscott as a fourth against the United States International Team. We won that match—I like winning—so I know first-hand what a fine player Alan is.

We lose occasionally, and agonize over the hand or two that turned the tide against us; and study the mistakes that cost us the match.

Yes, we know all too well that avoiding or minimizing mistakes is surely the secret to winning bridge. So I am pleased that a fine player and writer has now written a practical book on this vital subject.

Mark well Alan Truscott's words and your game will surely be improved.

OMAR SHARIF

Guidelines to Practical Bridge

WITHOUT QUESTION, bridge has become the most popular intellectual pastime in the world, with more than thirty million players in North America alone. The world total is perhaps double that; over fifty countries have national organizations devoted solely to the game. Bridge has far outdistanced chess; even the Russians, who regard playing cards as bourgeois capitalist instruments, now allow bridge tournaments.

The primary reason for bridge's pre-eminence is its universal appeal: it is open to both sexes, fun for all age levels and social classes, and stimulating to most intellects.

There are more women players than men, and they spend more time at the bridge table than their hard-working spouses simply because they have more time available. In tournaments, however, the numbers are equally balanced. The men win most of the trophies, and in the highest ranks they outnumber the ladies by about ten to one. Perhaps this is because men are more aggressive, and winning is more important to us.

The age-spread of bridge players is remarkable. An 11-year-old boy can play a respectable game, and so can a centenarian. A few years back, a sixth-grader named Kyle Larsen appeared in a National Championship playing quite competently with his father. Well before he was out of his teens, he was a national champion and is now one of America's top-rated players. The late George Beynon not only played bridge at the age of 100 but wrote a weekly newspaper column about the game and conducted a correspondence school for tournament directors; Harold Vanderbilt, who devised the present form of bridge back in 1925, continues to play a highly expert game in his mid-eighties.

Originally bridge was an upper-class game: Vanderbilt introduced it to high society, and for some years teams representing the men's social clubs of New York dominated the tournament scene. But the mass media and the general increase of leisure time have made the game popular among almost all occupational classes. Among the experts there are many lawyers, scientists, teachers, stockbrokers, businessmen, and—a recent development—computer programmers.

Only an average intelligence is required to play a decent game of bridge. If you can remember how to add and subtract—strictly second-grade stuff—you'll be all right.

Yet it is surprising how many players, with years of experience, continue to remain losers. They make the same mistakes now that they did years before. The most unfortunate part of it is that they do not recognize them.

Yet it need not be so. For individual brilliance, or even competence, has very little to do with winning bridge. Winning is simply a matter of making fewer mistakes than your opponents; the way to do that is to be sure to recognize your mistakes and to see that you do not repeat them. It is not the complicated hands that plague the consistent losers, but rather the simple ones they foul up in the bidding or mess up in play or defense. Even the experts have trouble with the complicated hands. Their edge is their sureness and care on the simple ones.

There are just two basic differences between the expert and the average player: the *number* and *type* of mistakes he makes.

An expert averages some five mistakes in twenty-six hands; the average player, about three times as many. (Some players are capable of making more mistakes than hands played; I have seen hands that resemble ping-pong games in that the advantage was thrown back and forth three or four times between the declarer and the defenders.)

An expert may consider it a mistake that he played a three of spades instead of a five, or that he failed to make a deceptive play; that he gave too much information in the bidding, or too little; that he played too boldly, or too cautiously.

The average player would never recognize what the expert considers to be a mistake; nor should he. *But the average player who does not recognize his own mistakes is a loser—and will remain one.*

With all the excellent books about bridge, it is remarkable that only a handful have singled out the one indispensable element for winning bridge—recognition and correction of the common mistakes.

This book is designed to do just that, and thereby enable the reader to get the most out of his cards—and out of his ability. It is the shortest and surest road to becoming a consistent winner in his own league.

HOW TO USE THIS BOOK

Just as an expert bridge player plans ahead before beginning the play of a hand, so, too, should you have a plan before reading this book.

Go step by step, building on the knowledge you already have. Take it slowly and build securely.

First, note the mistake commonly made by average bridge players; study the text until you understand clearly why it is a mistake, how to recognize it, and what measures to take to avoid repeating it.

Most of these common errors will be illustrated with a few examples, followed by a quiz that reinforces your learning and develops additional points.

Then, we will take you into some expert games to show you how top players approach the same situations. As you will see, even established champions sometimes go astray. Some of these hands may strike you as difficult, and indeed they are, simply because there is no easy way to become a winning bridge player.

This book will teach you not only the winning bids and plays, but also the bridge terms that describe them. There is a glossary beginning on page 213. If you are unfamiliar with a term when you first come across it, you will know you can look up the definition before reading on. However, if you already know the meaning of the term, you will be able to read on without interruption.

Thus, this book is a study course in many ways. The reward for applying yourself to it is the marked improvement it will make in your bridge game.

One of the most effective teaching techniques is to

lay out the North-South cards of a suit and sort out the remaining cards to East and West in different combinations until you are absolutely sure that the recommended bid or play works, and why.

Like nature, bridge is orderly and logical. As you read on, think of the logic of each situation, rather than memorizing rules or counting points. Even losers can memorize and count points; they are losers because this is precisely all they do at the bridge table. But *you* want to cut the number of your errors and become a regular winner. Right? Then read on.

GUIDE TO BASIC BIDDING

POINT COUNT

Count high cards according to the following scale:

Ace	=	4	Queen	=	2
King	=	3	Jack	=	1

An average hand will have . . . . 10 points
An average partnership will have . . . . 20 points
Total points in a deck. . . . . 40 points

DISTRIBUTION

There is an obvious advantage in having a long suit, and in a trump contract a short suit may be valuable, for the hand that is short may be able to ruff out losing cards in that suit.

Most players count points for distribution. There are two popular methods: valuing short suits and long suits. In the first, one extra point is counted for a doubleton, two for a singleton, and three for a void. Under the second method, an extra point is added for a 5-card suit, two for a 6-card suit, and so on.

In this book, the references to point count relate to high-card points without any addition for distributional strength, but distributional features should affect your high-card point-count valuation in the following way:

With a long suit, or two long suits	
With a good fit in partner's suit (four or more cards)	. . . . . . bid aggressively
With a bad fit for partner's suit (a singleton or a void)	. . . . . . bid cautiously

THE MAGIC NUMBERS

If you can judge that your partnership hands have a combined total of:

33 points . . . . bid a slam—after making sure that your side doesn't have two quick losers

26 points . . . . bid a game

Less than 26 points. . . . stop quickly in a part score

OPENING BIDS

1. *One of a suit:* Usually 13–20 points, but 12 points is acceptable with a 5-card suit, and 11 with a singleton or void and a 5-card or longer suit.

   (a) *Which suit to bid:* Normally, the longest available suit. With two or three suits of equal length, bid the suit as near as possible below the shortest suit. (Count spades as the suit below clubs.)

Try to avoid opening a feeble 4-card major suit, such as Q–x–x–x.

(b) *Rebids:* With 16–18 points, plan to bid strongly at the next opportunity. With 19–20, insist on game after any response from partner.

2. *One notrump:* 16–18 points and a balanced distribution (4-3-3-3, 4-4-3-2, or 5-3-3-2).

(a) *Responses:* The responder usually decides the right final contract immediately by passing or by bidding two of a suit, three notrump, four spades or four hearts, or six notrump.

The responder may invite a notrump game by bidding two notrump (showing 8 or 9 points) or a notrump slam by bidding four notrump (15–16 points).

The responder may look for a suit contract by jumping to three of a suit, showing a strong 5-card suit and an unbalanced hand, or by using the Stayman Convention (see page 16).

3. *Two of a suit* (the strong two bid): This guarantees a game contract and therefore shows great strength, normally more than 20 points. Points are less important than trick-taking power: the two-bidder promises game—or within one trick of game—all in his own hand.

(a) *Responses:* With a weak hand—less than 7 points in aces and kings—responder bids two notrump, an artificial and negative response.

(Any other bid is positive, indicating 7 or more points.) In either case, the bidding must continue until game is reached.

4. *Two notrump:* 22–23 points and a balanced distribution. (A three notrump bid is 2–3 points stronger.)

5. *Three or more in a suit* (pre-emptive bids): A long, strong suit of seven or more cards with little strength in the other suits. The point count is usually less than 12. (Tournament players use about the same treatment for bids of two spades, hearts, or diamonds, except that these usually show 6-card suits.)

RESPONDING TO A BID OF ONE OF A SUIT

Always respond with 6 or more points. The choices are:

1. *One of a suit:* Requires 6 or more points with at least four cards in the suit bid. Normally, you bid the longest available suit. With suits of equal length: bid the lowest-ranking 4-card suit if you can do so at the one-level. Bid the higher-ranking of two 5-card suits. Unless responder has passed originally, opener must bid again.

2. *One notrump:* Requires 6–9 points. Avoid this response if you hold a 4-card suit that can be bid at the one-level or if you have support for partner's suit.

3. *Two of a lower ranking suit:* Requires 10 or more points and at least four cards in the suit bid (five cards for a two-heart response over one spade, or if you have passed originally).

4. *Two of partner's suit:* Requires 6–9 points and preferably four cards in partner's suit. 3-card support is permissible if partner's suit is a major and you have other than 4–3–3–3 distribution.

5. *Two notrump:* Requires 13–15 points and balanced distribution. This response commits the partnership to game.

6. *Jump in a new suit* (such as one heart—two spades, or one heart—three clubs): This is the strongest possible response, promising at least 17 points and looking toward slam. The hand must also have a long strong suit or a good fit with the opener's suit.

7. *Three of partner's suit:* Requires 13–16 points and at least four cards in opener's suit. It commits the partnership to game.

8. *Three notrump:* Requires 16–18 points, stoppers in all unbid suits, and a balanced distribution.

9. *Double jump in a new suit* (such as one heart—three spades, or one heart—four clubs): A long broken suit with little outside strength. This is a rarely used pre-emptive call.

10. *Four of partner's major suit:* Requires 7–12 points, at least 4-card support, and a singleton or a void somewhere.

CONVENTIONS

There are two conventions used by almost all bridge players:

1. *Blackwood:* After a suit fit has been revealed, a bid of four notrump is an artificial request to partner to reveal the number of aces he holds.

The responses are:

With no aces or four aces . . . . five clubs
With one ace . . . . five diamonds
With two aces. . . . . five hearts
With three aces. . . . . five spades

If the four notrump bidder continues with five notrump, he asks for kings in the same manner and promises possession of all four aces.

Not every four-notrump bid asks for aces. If no suit fit is evident, for example, one notrump–four notrump, it is a natural invitation to partner to bid six notrump.

2. *Stayman:* A bid of two clubs in response to one notrump is an artificial bid requesting opener to show a 4-card major suit if he can, for game in a 4–4 major suit may play better than at three notrump. Responder suggests four cards in at least one major when he responds two clubs.

Opener dutifully bids his 4-card major if he has one; if he has 4-card holdings in both majors, he bids two spades (or two hearts, depending upon the partnership understanding); if he lacks a 4-card major suit, opener makes the artificial bid of two diamonds.

With a weak hand containing six or more clubs, responder first bids two clubs and then follows with three clubs, which asks opener to pass him out at that contract.

DEFENSIVE BIDDING

There are several actions possible when the right-hand opponent bids one of a suit:

1. *A simple overcall in a suit* (East: one heart, South: one spade): This shows at least a 5-card suit and about the strength for an opening bid.

2. *A one-notrump overcall* (East: one heart, South: one notrump): This describes a hand that could open one notrump: 16–18 points and balanced distribution.

3. *A jump overcall in a suit* (East: one heart, South: two spades): Traditionally, this shows a strong hand with 15–18 points, but most experienced players now use it to show a weak hand with less than the strength for an opening bid. (Discuss this in advance with your partner.)

4. *A bid in the opponent's suit* (East: one spade, South: two spades): This is called a cue bid and is the strongest possible action after the opponents have opened the bidding. Like the strong opening two-bid, it demands that the partnership reach game.

   However, if partner has already bid or doubled, the cue bid in the opponent's suit asks partner to describe his hand further and forces him to make at least one more bid. At a high level, with a slam in view, the cue bid promises first-round control—ace or void—of the opponent's suit.

5. *A double:* Called a takeout double, this call indicates about the strength for an opening bid, and it suggests that the doubler holds three or more cards in each unbid suit. He may be shorter than this in the unbid suits and still double, provided his hand is otherwise much stronger than a normal opening of one in a suit.

(a) *Responses:* A jump in an unbid suit shows about 10 points. A cue bid in the opponent's suit indicates 13 or more points.

(b) *Action by the opener's partner:* A redouble promises 10 points or more; any other action shows less than 10 points.

(c) *Other takeout doubles:* Doubles of other suit bids at a low level are also for takeout if partner has not bid.

GUIDE TO BASIC PLAY AND DEFENSE

PLAY

In managing his own hand and the dummy, declarer should apply the following general principles:

1. Lead from low cards toward high cards.

2. When your side has all or nearly all the high cards in a suit, play off the high honors first from the hand that is shorter in that suit.

3. Play the lowest *significant* high card (K–J–x, A–Q–**10**, A–Q–**9**, Q–**10**–x, A–J–**9)** when you lead toward high cards. (When you hope that the opposing honor cards are located in front of your high cards, you are finessing.)

4. Do not be in a hurry to lead out aces and kings; save them for control later.

5. Surrender graciously and quickly those tricks that must be lost eventually.

In notrump contracts:

6. Attack the suit in which your side holds the most cards. Do not rush to take tricks in a suit with obvious winners and no losers.

7. Do not be in a hurry to take a sure trick in the opponent's long, strong suit.

8. Count your sure tricks and then search for the remaining tricks you need.

In trump contracts:

9. Count the opponent's trumps as they appear and keep track of the number and ranking of the unplayed ones.

10. Play for ruffs when dummy has a short suit in which you have losers.

11. Delay drawing trumps if the trump suit provides needed entries to either hand or if you are in danger of losing control of the hand.

12. Otherwise, draw the opposing trumps at once.

13. Count the likely losing tricks. If the total is enough to spell defeat to the contract, look for a way to avoid a loser or two.

DEFENSE

1. Against a notrump contract, open from your long suit if you have entry cards; otherwise, open an unbid short suit and hope you hit partner's long suit.

2. Lead a well-supported honor card or a card in a worthless suit against a trump contract.

3. If you are third to play to a trick, play your highest card, except when you want to save it to capture an honor in dummy later.

4. If you are second to play to a trick, play your lowest card ("second hand low") unless you have a good reason not to.

5. With two or three high cards in sequence (a) lead

the top card of the sequence but (b) follow suit with the lowest card.

6. Avoid leading a suit in which you have prospects of capturing a high card in the hand to your right.

7. Avoid leading out aces and kings: use them instead to capture lower honors so they retain their power.

8. Don't rush in to take a sure trick in dummy's long, strong suit; if you wait, you may prevent declarer from running that suit.

9. If the declarer leads an unsupported honor from dummy—or what might be an unsupported honor from his own hand—and you are next to play, cover with a higher honor if you think it may promote a trick for yourself or your partner. It is usually wrong to cover if the other defender is likely to be short in the suit.

10. Play an unnecessarily high card to tell your partner "lead this suit." When signaling in this way, play the highest card you can spare.

11. In a trump contract, consider leading a trump if dummy has ruffing prospects and the declarer is avoiding trump leads.

PART I

Mistakes in Bidding

Mistakes in Bidding

THOUGHTLESS REBIDDING
OF 5-CARD SUITS

MOST TEXTBOOKS assure you that you can bid and rebid any 5-card suit that is headed by two honors. What they neglect to point out is that it is nearly always wrong to do so.

Remember that you are aiming for a trump suit of eight cards in the two combined hands. A 7-card fit is sometimes playable, but anything less is likely to be a catastrophe, for your opponents will then have the majority of the trumps.

How many times have you opened one spade and then rebid two spades with something like A–Q–9–3–2, only to hear your partner pass holding a singleton or even a void in spades. Precisely this situation cost the American team 950 points in the World Championship match against Italy in 1959 (see page 30).

In this particular match, the American players opened and rebid in the same suit eighteen times. Once, the suit was a 7-carder; thirteen times it was six cards in length; only four times was a 5-card suit rebid! And, of these four occasions, once the suit was overwhelmingly strong (A–K–Q–10–x), and twice the rebid was imposed on the player by his bidding system; it was not a choice he would have made voluntarily.

Putting aside systemic demands, the rebid of the same suit showed a 6-card suit fourteen times out of sixteen; this would be typical in any expert match.

If the experts avoid rebidding 5-card suits like the plague, shouldn't you?

Of course you should, but you would be the exception. For on any given day throughout the land, millions of players continue to bid and rebid moth-eaten 5-card suits and are blissfully unaware that they are in error.

The usual alibi goes like this: "I had to rebid the suit to show you I had a 5-card suit." Sheer nonsense. Sooner or later, opener's partner is likely to support the suit if he has as many as three cards in it. If he does not give support, it probably means that he has, at most, two cards, for a partnership total of seven, at best.

There is ample evidence to prove that players generally stumble and lose control unless they have a trump holding of eight cards or more between the two hands. For example:

WEST   EAST

♡ Q 10 8 5 2   ♡ 6

With this as a trump suit, West is almost sure to lose four trump tricks. Clearly he would be better off in notrump or another suit.

Of course, West's suit was anemic in this example. With a stronger suit, there is more to be said for rebidding it. The more honor cards the better: three is usually adequate, but it helps to have a nine or eight to boot:

WEST	EAST
♡ Q J 10 8 4	♡ 6

Here, there are only two *clear-cut* losers, but you would be surprised how often they become four. If this is your trump suit, your best play for three tricks may be to ruff with the four and the eight or to wait for the opponents to lead to you. But you may have to draw trumps to protect your winners in other suits; in that case, the right play, surprisingly, is to lead the six and finesse the eight on the first round.

A couple of common-sense rules will eliminate your temptation to rebid unsoundly:

1. *Never rebid a weak 5-card suit.* Just visualize your partner with a singleton in your suit and it will strengthen your resolve.
2. *Never rebid a 5-card suit if there is a sensible alternative.* Let's apply this second rule to a specific case. You hold:

    ♠ K 5 4   ♡ K J 10 6 5   ◇ 8 7   ♣ A Q 7

    You open one heart, determined that you will not rebid hearts if you can help it. How well will you keep your resolution if your partner responds:
    One Spade? Simply raise to two spades; you can support partner's first bid major with three cards.
    One Notrump? Pass; your hand is balanced and his bid is not forcing.
    Two Clubs? Raise to three clubs; partner is likely to have five clubs; even if he has only four, his hand is probably strong enough for a further bid.
    Two Diamonds? Now you must reluctantly rebid

your hearts for want of any sensible alternative. Even in this case, some players would venture two notrump; others would make the same bid without trepidation if they had an understanding with their partners that this rebid does not show any extra values over a minimum opening bid.

From these examples it follows that opener's immediate rebid in the same suit normally shows six cards unless responder is known to have some support for the suit or unless a forcing situation exists. Exceptions should be rare.

Now, test yourself on the following hands:

REBIDDING QUIZ

Neither side is vulnerable.

1. YOUR HAND:	You open the bidding with
♠ A K J 8 5	one spade. What would you
♡ K 7 2	rebid if your partner responds:
◇ Q 9 4	(a) 2 ♡ (c) 2 ♣
♣ 6 5	(b) 2 ◇ (d) 1 NT

2. YOUR HAND:	You open the bidding with
♠ Q 8 7 4 3	one spade. What would you
♡ 8 6 2	rebid if your partner responds:
◇ A K 5	(a) 2 ♡ (c) 2 ♣
♣ A 3	(b) 2 ◇ (d) 1 NT

3. YOUR HAND:	You open the bidding with
♠ A	one diamond. What would you
♡ Q 8 6 3	rebid if your partner responds:
◇ K 10 6 5 2	(a) 1 ♡ (c) 1 NT
♣ A 7 3	(b) 1 ♠ (d) 2 ♣

4. YOUR HAND:
   ♠ J 2
   ♡ A J 8 7 4
   ◇ 9 6 3
   ♣ 6 5 2

Your partner opens the bidding with one diamond and you respond one heart. What would your next bid be if your partner rebids:

(a) 1 ♠   (c) 2 ♣
(b) 1 NT   (d) 3 ♣

5. YOUR HAND:
   ♠ 8 4
   ♡ A Q 6 4 3
   ◇ K Q 2
   ♣ 9 8 5

Your right-hand opponent opens the bidding with one club and from then on the opponents are silent. You overcall one heart. What would you do next if your partner bids:

(a) 1 ♠   (c) 2 ♣
(b) 1 NT   (d) 3 ♡

ANSWERS TO REBIDDING QUIZ

1. (a) *Three hearts.* A response of two hearts to one spade promises at least a 5-card heart suit, so the combined hands must have at least eight hearts.

   (b) *Three diamonds.* A diamond fit is guaranteed but a spade fit is not. Partner should have at least five diamonds or a hand worth a second bid. If he passes three diamonds, the contract will be sound.

   (c) *Two spades.* You rebid the 5-card suit for want of anything better. Two notrump is also acceptable if your partner will understand that you have a minimum hand. (In standard methods, the two notrump rebid would show about 15 points.)

(d) *Pass.* Without any question. Partner is unlikely to have more than a doubleton spade, and a rebid of two spades would guarantee at least a 6-card suit.

2. (a) *Three hearts.* As before, an 8-card fit is known and the lack of a heart honor should not deter you. If you can fit your partner's suit, tell him.

(b) *Three diamonds.* An obvious one.

(c) *Two diamonds.* We cannot support clubs, rebid the bad spade suit, nor bid notrump. A bid in a strong 3-card suit is often the least evil.

(d) *Pass.* Easy.

3. (a) *Two hearts.* The good fit and the singleton make it tempting to bid three hearts, but a good game is unlikely if partner passes over two hearts. He probably has some wasted strength in spades, since the opponents did not overcall in that suit.

(b) *One notrump.* A notrump rebid with a singleton in partner's suit is often the best way out of this dilemma. Even two clubs would be better than two diamonds (for the suit is so weak) or two hearts (a reverse bid showing a strong hand).

(c) *Two clubs.* Partner surely has at least four clubs and probably has five or six, since he could not bid hearts or spades or raise diamonds. With three diamonds and four clubs he is likely to return to two diamonds. You should not pass to one notrump because of the serious spade weakness, but two diamonds is a fair alternative.

(d) *Three clubs.* Descriptive, and does not promise more than a minimum.

4. (a) *Two diamonds.* A simple preference bid. To pass would be wrong because your partner would be playing with a 4–2 trump fit. You cannot rebid the poor 5-card heart suit, nor bid notrump without a club stopper.

(b) *Pass.* And let him struggle. But as the spade suit will be weak, two diamonds is an acceptable alternative giving partner the option of going to two hearts. A two-heart bid on your own would be inferior.

(c) *Two diamonds.* A simple preference bid. The opener should have at least five diamonds and at least four clubs, so return to the suit which is likely to be longer and does not raise the level. No marks for a pass or for two hearts.

(d) *Three diamonds.* Partner has promised game, but there is no need to emphasize hearts unduly by bidding them again. If he has 3-card support for you, he will bid three hearts over three diamonds.

5. (a) *Pass.* A new suit bid is not forcing when the opponents have opened the bidding. Partner presumably has at least five spades and lacks heart support. Game prospects are negligible.

(b) *Pass.* One notrump is an encouraging response

to an overcall, but it denies support in partner's suit; game prospects are negligible.

(c) *Two diamonds.* Partner's cue bid in clubs suggests, but does not guarantee, a game. By
showing something in diamonds you may help
him to bid game in notrump. A heart rebid
would not enlighten him.

(d) *Pass.* All jump bids are invitational—that is,
not forcing—when the opponents have opened
the bidding. This hand is a minimum overcall, and the holding of three small cards in
the opponent's suit is a danger signal.

Now watch the experts in action:

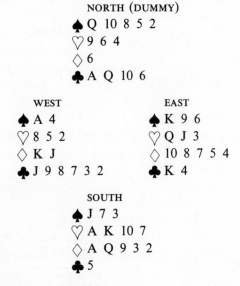

```
                NORTH (DUMMY)
                ♠ Q 10 8 5 2
                ♡ 9 6 4
                ◇ 6
                ♣ A Q 10 6

   WEST                        EAST
   ♠ A 4                       ♠ K 9 6
   ♡ 8 5 2                     ♡ Q J 3
   ◇ K J                       ◇ 10 8 7 5 4
   ♣ J 9 8 7 3 2               ♣ K 4

                SOUTH
                ♠ J 7 3
                ♡ A K 10 7
                ◇ A Q 9 3 2
                ♣ 5
```

Both sides vulnerable.

Table 1:

SOUTH	NORTH
(U.S.A.)	(U.S.A.)
1 ♦	1 ♠
2 ♦	All pass

Table 2:

SOUTH	NORTH
(Italy)	(Italy)
1 ♡	1 ♠
2 ♠	3 ♠
4 ♠	All pass

When this hand occurred in the 1959 World Championship, the American pair reached the terrible contract of two diamonds as shown in the diagram. The traditional opening bid with the South hand is one heart, but North-South's system barred an opening bid in a 4-card major suit. It was South's second bid that was fatal: he rebid his 5-card suit when he could and should have supported his partner. If your partner responds in a major, you can support him with three cards without qualms.

South fared badly at two diamonds; he finessed the club queen at the first trick, losing to the king. The heart three was returned and South won with the ace. He attacked spades; West put up the ace and continued the suit, ruffing the third round. The diamond king was led and taken by the ace, and there was now no possible way to avoid the loss of a heart and two trumps.

The Italian South sensibly opened the bidding with

one heart, raised his partner's one-spade response, and finally continued to game in spades.

Four spades was a slightly optimistic contract, and would probably have been defeated if East had chosen to lead a trump. The defenders could then have removed dummy's trumps immediately, and North could only have made ten tricks by inspired guessing. In fact, however, East led a diamond and the ace won in dummy. A diamond ruff, the club ace, and a club ruff won the next three tricks, and the diamond queen was led. West and North both discarded hearts. After cashing his heart winners, North continued the cross-ruff, making eleven tricks.

Italy gained a huge swing largely attributable to the Americans' unwise rebid of the 5-card diamond suit.

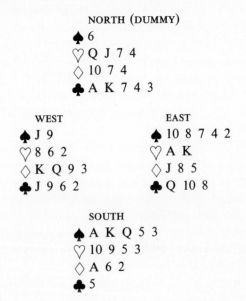

NORTH (DUMMY)
♠ 6
♡ Q J 7 4
♢ 10 7 4
♣ A K 7 4 3

WEST
♠ J 9
♡ 8 6 2
♢ K Q 9 3
♣ J 9 6 2

EAST
♠ 10 8 7 4 2
♡ A K
♢ J 8 5
♣ Q 10 8

SOUTH
♠ A K Q 5 3
♡ 10 9 5 3
♢ A 6 2
♣ 5

Both sides vulnerable.

SOUTH	WEST	NORTH	EAST
1 ♠	Pass	2 ♣	Pass
2 ♡	Pass	3 ♡	Pass
4 ♡	All pass		

As often happens, the opener's second bid was the turning point on this deal. If he had mistakenly bid two spades, lured by the strength of the spade suit and frowning upon the weakness of the hearts, the bidding would have ended there. But South appreciated, as many average players do not, that a bid of a new, lower ranking suit shows no more strength than a rebid of his first suit.

Four hearts is an excellent contract, and was reached because South rebid intelligently. With normal breaks the game would be made easily, but the bad spade break is a nuisance as the cards lie.

West did his best by leading a trump, and South was fortunate that the defenders were unable to lead a third round. He would then have had to rely entirely on a 4–3 spade division.

East took two trump tricks and shifted to a diamond, taken by South's ace. If South had attacked spades immediately, expecting the suit to break, he would have gone down. Instead he cashed two rounds of clubs, discarding a diamond, then ruffed a club, and played three top spades. West was able to ruff, but dummy over-ruffed and the fifth club was established while a trump entry remained on the board.

It would not have helped West to discard on the

third spade, for South could then cross-ruff with high trumps for the three additional tricks he needed.

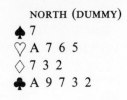

NORTH (DUMMY)
♠ 7
♡ A 7 6 5
♢ 7 3 2
♣ A 9 7 3 2

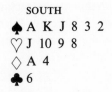

WEST
♠ 10 9
♡ K Q 3
♢ K 10 6
♣ Q J 10 5 4

EAST
♠ Q 6 5 4
♡ 4 2
♢ Q J 9 8 5
♣ K 8

SOUTH
♠ A K J 8 3 2
♡ J 10 9 8
♢ A 4
♣ 6

East-West vulnerable.

EAST	SOUTH	WEST	NORTH
Pass	1 ♠	Pass	1 NT
Pass	2 ♠	All pass	

Bidding a suit twice should nearly always show a 6-card suit, but it does not follow that a 6-card suit *must* be rebid immediately. It will sometimes be better to show a 4-card major on the second round.

The bidding shown in the diagram was produced by

an expert pair and is "standard." Nevertheless, there is much to be said for a rebid of two hearts, and one expert who made that bid in a bidding contest was able to reach the excellent contract of four hearts. He saw that the heart fit had to be explored immediately and that he might well have a chance to rebid spades later, thus implying 6–4 distribution.

This deal was originally played in the 1954 World Championship. Both North players responded two clubs with the North hand—an over-aggressive action by modern standards (most experts would choose a one-notrump response). Even so, four hearts was not reached because neither South player thought fit to bid his hearts. One bid three spades and the other two spades, ending the auction in each case.

As it happens, game in hearts is easily made; yet only one imaginative expert led his partnership there.

EXCESSIVE EXPLORATION

In the early days of bridge, bidding was bold and an adventurous spirit prevailed. Those hardy pioneers simply bid what they thought they could make and had no patience to "fool around" with fancy, exploratory bids that might reveal something of partner's holding.

Then, the pendulum swung in the opposite direction. "Scientific" bidding came into its own. A delicate exchange of bids became the accepted means of reaching the final contract.

There's something to be said for both schools: taking charge of the bidding may easily land the partnership in the wrong spot, but it certainly keeps the opponents in the dark; exploratory bidding is more accurate, but it gives the defenders a great deal of useful information about their opponents' hands.

The trouble with most players is that they do not know when to explore and when to leap. They generally err in the modern mode by taking as many bids as possible to arrive at a final contract. This not only aids the opponents on defense, it frequently confuses partner.

So, if you know where you want to play the hand, just go ahead and bid it and enjoy yourself. But explore when you are not sure where you are heading. In general, you'll do better by reaching your contract quickly.

The more descriptive your opening bid, the greater your chance for a quick auction. Over a one-notrump opening, for example, responder can usually place the final contract immediately. If he passes, bids two of a suit naturally, or jumps to game, opener will usually take no further action. Whenever he can, responder should take this direct route, choosing one of these options.

Consider these two hands after your partner opens one heart:

(a) ♠ K Q x x ♡ J x x x ◇ J x x ♣ x x
(b) ♠ K Q x x ♡ A J x x ◇ K x x ♣ x x

In both cases, it is a mistake to make the "automatic" response of one spade. Not only is it a roundabout bid, concealing the chief strength of your hand —the heart support—but it gives your left-hand opponent a cheap chance to make a takeout double or a low-level overcall.

On (a), raise to two hearts. You know there is a heart fit and that the hand should play in hearts, so let partner in on the secret. If you first bid spades and then support hearts, he will suspect that you have but 3-card support.

On (b), raise immediately to three hearts. This shows strong heart support and guarantees a game, whereas a one-spade response tells your partner very little.

The advantages of direct bidding apply with equal force to your *second* bid:

♠ x x   ♡ K J 10 x   ◇ K x   ♣ A Q x x x

You sit North with this hand; the bidding is:

SOUTH	NORTH
1 ♠	2 ♣
2 ◇	?

At this point, you know you want to play in three notrump, right? Well, then, bid it. Why mess around with a wishy-washy two-heart rebid when you want to be in notrump?

What terrible thing will happen if you bid two hearts? Well, there are two possibilities: first, partner may read you for an unbalanced hand (otherwise you would have bid notrump) and may take you out of notrump, if you later bid it, into one of your suits where he has grudging support.

In an expert game, you run a second risk: you have bid fourth suit forcing: you have shown the fourth suit after the partnership has bid the other three. Many experts play this as a forcing waiting bid, asking partner to describe his hand more fully. Partner will doubt that you really have hearts ("why didn't you bid notrump when you had the hearts stopped?" he'll ask later), so he will assume you are requesting him to bid notrump if he has a heart stopper. If the partnership survives this muddle it will be lucky.

EXPLORATION QUIZ

Neither side is vulnerable.

1. Your partner opens the bidding with one notrump, showing a balanced hand with 16–18 points. What would you respond with each of the following hands:

   (a) ♠ 9 8 6 4 3 2   ♡ 5   ◇ 10 6 3   ♣ 8 7 4

   (b) ♠ K J 9 8 6 4   ♡ 5   ◇ 10 6 3   ♣ A 8 7

   (c) ♠ 8 5   ♡ 10 3   ◇ A K 7 6 2   ♣ K 8 6 5

   (d) ♠ K 8 5   ♡ 2   ◇ A K 7 6 2   ♣ Q 8 6 5

   (e) ♠ K 9 8 3   ♡ Q 8 6 2   ◇ 5   ♣ K 5 3 2

   (f) ♠ A K 3   ♡ Q J 7   ◇ A Q J   ♣ 9 8 3 2

2. You have the following hand:

   ♠ J 7 4 3   ♡ K 7 5 2   ◇ A Q   ♣ K 9 5

   What should you respond if your partner opens:

       (a) 1 ♣   (b) 1 ♡   (c) 1 NT

3. You have the following hand:

   ♠ K J 5 4   ♡ 6 4   ◇ A K J 4   ♣ Q 8 2

   The bidding goes: PARTNER   YOU

                              1 ♣   1 ◇

What would your next bid be if your partner rebids:

(a) 1 ♡   (b) 1 ♠   (c) 1 NT   (d) 2 ◇

4. The bidding:

PARTNER	YOU
1 ♠	2 ♣
2 ♡	?

What should you bid now with these hands:

(a) ♠ 6   ♡ J 8 5   ◇ K J 10 8   ♣ A K J 7 2

(b) ♠ K J 7 3   ♡ 8 6   ◇ 5 3   ♣ A K J 7 2

(c) ♠ K 7   ♡ K 8 4 3   ◇ 5 2   ♣ A Q 10 6 2

(d) ♠ 6 5   ♡ K 4   ◇ 7 6 3   ♣ A K Q J 5 2

ANSWERS TO EXPLORATION QUIZ

1. (a) *Two spades.* A command to your partner to pass. Your bid announces that the partnership assets are insufficient for game and that two spades will be more productive than one notrump. You promise at least five spades and at most 6 high-card points.

   (b) *Four spades.* You know the combined hands have at least eight spades. There should be a play for ten tricks, but no prospect for twelve. As you know what the contract should be, it would be pointless to bid three spades, which asks about spade support. A Stayman bid of two clubs would give away useful information to the opponents without any matching gain for your side.

   (c) *Three notrump.* The combined strength is enough for game and there is no reason to look beyond three notrump. A jump to three diamonds* would unjustifiably suggest slam possibilities and might help the opponents to find the best lead against three notrump.

(d) *Three diamonds.* * Now there is a prospect of slam if the hands fit well, and game in a suit may be right if the opener is weak in hearts. The intention here is to bid three notrump over a three-heart rebid, otherwise to continue to game or slam in a suit.

(e) *Two clubs.* The Stayman convention, asking the opener to bid a 4-card major suit. If he bids two spades or two hearts, invite game by raising to the three-level. If he bids two diamonds, an artificial bid denying a major, bid two notrump and leave him the option of bidding game.

(f) *Six notrump.* The combined hands have at least 33 points, which is enough for six notrump. There is no reason to look for a suit contract, and the chance of a sound grand slam is remote, so bid the slam immediately.

2. (a) *One heart.* This hand *does* need exploration, for there may be a 4–4 fit in a major suit. With two 4-card suits responder should usually make the most economical response; here, one heart gives opener a chance to bid spades if he has that suit. A response of two notrump

---

* Many experts now play a three-club or three-diamond response to a one-notrump opening as a weak, pre-emptive bid. They bid two clubs, Stayman, and follow with a rebid of three clubs (or diamonds) to indicate the strong hand interested in slam.

deserves some credit, for it conceals the distribution from your opponents.

(b) *Three hearts.* This is the standard way of showing an opening bid with at least 4-card support for opener's suit. It would be pointless to bid one spade or two notrump once the partnership is known to have an 8-card heart fit and a four-heart response would mislead partner by indicating much less in high-card strength and better distribution.

(c) *Three notrump.* This contract must be safe, and there is no prospect of a slam. The use of a Stayman two-club response in the hope of playing in a 4-4 fit in spades or hearts unnecessarily runs the slight risk of hitting a 5-0 trump break. (However, two clubs would be acceptable at duplicate scoring.)

3. (a) *Three notrump.* There is nothing to be gained from bidding one spade. Even if partner has four spades, which is just possible, the notrump game should be equally good. Take credit for two notrump, but remember that many good players would treat such a jump as invitational, not forcing. Unless you know your partner well, you should not run the risk that he will pass to two notrump.

(b) *Four spades.* Again, you can bid the game directly, and the same comment applies. Many experts would regard a jump to three spades as a non-forcing invitation to game. If you have a regular partner, discuss this point with him.

(c) *Three notrump.* Your partner would have bid one spade if he had four of them. Thus, there is no spade fit and notrump is the shortest road to game. At three notrump, your partner may be embarrassed by a heart lead, but you cannot help that.

(d) *Two spades.* Your partner presumably has four diamonds and at least four clubs. If he has a heart stopper, he can now bid notrump, and three notrump will be the final contract. If he cannot stop hearts you will have to play five diamonds, or perhaps even four spades.

4. (a) *Three notrump.* The combined hands have the necessary point count values for a game, and it is most unlikely that a suit will play better than notrump. A bid of three diamonds would leave you wandering in outer darkness if your partner raised diamonds or put you back to clubs. Do not expect him to bid three notrump automatically, for a bid of three diamonds might mean he is weak in diamonds—see (d) below.

(b) *Four spades.* This completes the description of your hand and makes it clear that you have 4-card support for spades. A jump to three spades would give the impression of 3-card spade support.

(c) *Four hearts.* An easy one. You want to be in game so do not bid three hearts, which your partner might pass. All your high cards look useful, and the spade doubleton may help him establish the suit.

(d) *Three diamonds.* There is no satisfactory natural bid. Three clubs would indicate a much weaker hand and would probably be passed. Four clubs or five clubs would get you past three notrump, which will be the right final contract if partner can stop diamonds. This is the implicit convention called fourth-suit forcing. The opener should not assume the fourth suit is a genuine one, and must not bid notrump unless he stops the suit himself. If responder really has diamonds, as in (a), he will bid notrump himself, so failure to bid notrump suggests a diamond weakness.

Now, let us kibitz the experts again:

NORTH (DUMMY)
♠ J 8 6 3
♡ K 9
♢ K Q 6 5
♣ J 7 3

WEST
♠ K 10 4
♡ 10 8 5
♢ A 9 4 3 2
♣ K 5

EAST
♠ A 9 5 2
♡ 7 6 4 2
♢ 7
♣ 10 9 6 4

SOUTH
♠ Q 7
♡ A Q J 3
♢ J 10 8
♣ A Q 8 2

North-South vulnerable.

NORTH	EAST	SOUTH	WEST
Pass	Pass	1 NT	Pass
2 ♣	Pass	2 ♡	Pass
3 NT	Pass	All pass	

When this hand was played in a New York tournament, some South players made the mistake of opening one heart without looking ahead. North correctly
responded one spade, and South had an awkward rebid. One notrump seemed the least misleading action,
but it was an underbid suggesting 13–15 points, not
16, and North had no reason to bid again. A sound
game contract was missed.

One notrump was South's proper opening bid despite the weakness in spades and diamonds, for any
other opening presents a problem in rebidding, as we
have seen.

After the one-notrump opening, North comfortably
bids game in notrump after exploring, via Stayman,
for a 4–4 spade fit.

At three notrump, South won the opening diamond
lead with the eight and continued with the jack. West
rightly ducked and South had a problem.

A third diamond lead would give West a chance to
win and return a fourth round of the suit, thus setting up his last diamond. Eventually, East-West might
take two spades, two diamonds, and a club before
South could take nine tricks. If declarer crossed to
dummy with the heart king in order to take a club
finesse, he might never be able to get back to dummy
to cash the fourth diamond.

The solution is to set up a club trick before resuming diamonds. This nets declarer four hearts, two clubs, three diamonds—and his contract. Leading the club queen at the third trick is the simple way; declarer could also have led to the club jack, but then he would have had to be careful to win a heart return in his own hand so as to preserve the heart king as entry for the fourth diamond.

It would be wrong to cash the club ace at the third trick. If one of the opponents held K–10–9–x in clubs, he could win with the king and continue the suit, establishing the fifth and setting trick in clubs.

Thus, the only sure road to nine tricks against any distribution was to play the club queen (or a low club to the jack) at the third trick.

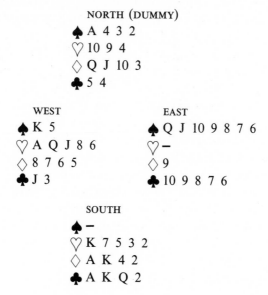

```
                NORTH (DUMMY)
                ♠ A 4 3 2
                ♡ 10 9 4
                ◇ Q J 10 3
                ♣ 5 4

     WEST                    EAST
   ♠ K 5                   ♠ Q J 10 9 8 7 6
   ♡ A Q J 8 6             ♡ —
   ◇ 8 7 6 5               ◇ 9
   ♣ J 3                   ♣ 10 9 8 7 6

                SOUTH
                ♠ —
                ♡ K 7 5 3 2
                ◇ A K 4 2
                ♣ A K Q 2
```

Neither side vulnerable.

NORTH	EAST	SOUTH	WEST
Pass	Pass	1 ♡	Pass
2 ♡	3 ♠	4 ♡	Dbl.
All pass			

There would be no story to tell if East had properly opened with a pre-emptive call of three spades.
Certainly, he had an ideal hand for trying to shut the
opponents out of the bidding—great playing strength
in spades and no defensive values. Had he bid three
spades at his first opportunity, North-South would
have had to be clairvoyant to get to their excellent
heart game.

As it was, the second round was too late to cause
North-South any trouble, for they had already found
their heart fit, thanks to North's good judgment. Most
players in North's shoes would automatically respond
one spade to their partner's opening one-heart bid—
"showing the other major" and all that. But North
rightly saw no sense in going on an exploratory jour-
ney. "I have heart support, so I'd better show it now,
for I might not get a chance later; besides, my hand
is worth just one bid, so I'll make the one that will
be most helpful to my partner."

How right he was. Looking just at the North-South
hands, four hearts is an excellent contract. Even with
the actual trump split, South was able to bring home
his game, for West's greedy double had tipped him off
to the winning line of play.

West led the spade king and declarer won with

dummy's ace, discarding a club from his hand. Warned by the double, he left the trump suit alone and played two top clubs and four winning diamonds, ending with the lead in his hand in this position:

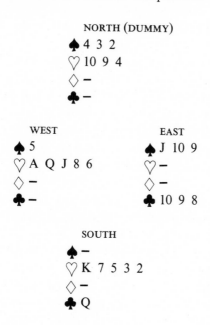

NORTH (DUMMY)
♠ 4 3 2
♡ 10 9 4
♢ –
♣ –

WEST
♠ 5
♡ A Q J 8 6
♢ –
♣ –

EAST
♠ J 10 9
♡ –
♢ –
♣ 10 9 8

SOUTH
♠ –
♡ K 7 5 3 2
♢ –
♣ Q

South then led the club queen, and no matter how West twisted and turned, he could not make more than three tricks.

Without the revealing double, South would no doubt have led one round of trumps and been defeated. West could then have won the first trump lead and played two more high trumps, forcing South's king and leaving himself with the eight-six as sure winners over South's seven-five.

MISUSE OF BLACKWOOD

Beginners quickly learn that if partner bids four notrump he is asking about aces, and that a response of five clubs means no ace (or all four aces); a response of five diamonds, one ace; and so on. Somehow, they also get the notion that it is a sin to bid a slam without using the Blackwood Convention. Oddly enough, Blackwood was devised to keep them out of unmakeable slams.

But there is a good deal more to it than that. There are some problems in responding to Blackwood, and others in deciding what to do after the response. Most important of all is the decision whether or not to bid Blackwood in the first place. Consider these points:

1. *Do your combined hands seem to have sufficient strength for slam, counting the high cards and distribution?* If this seems doubtful, do not use Blackwood. Regard Blackwood as a means of putting on the brakes when a slam seems promising but two aces are missing. Remember that there are other roads to slam. Once a suit fit has been found, any bid in another suit above the game level or immediately below the game level will suggest a slam.

2. *Do you have aces or kings?* If aces, you will probably be wiser to hint at a slam and let your partner use Blackwood and make the decisions. The ideal Blackwood hand is one with a wealth of second-round controls—kings and singletons.

3. *Do you have a void?* If so, do not use Blackwood. Unless your partner shows all the missing aces,

you will not know what to do next; the ace of your void suit will not help you, but the other aces will. Blackwood will tell you only *how many* aces partner has, but not *which ones.*

4. *Do you have two or more immediate losers in an unbid suit?* If so, avoid Blackwood. If you find there is one ace missing, you will not know what to do on the next round. Find another way to move toward slam.

5. *Do you have a weak hand opposite a very strong one?* If so, leave Blackwood to your partner. The weak hand is badly placed to make decisions, and so should not take charge of the auction.

6. *Are you sure your four-notrump bid will be understood as Blackwood?* If nobody has bid a suit, four notrump is a natural invitation to six notrump. And experts play many four-notrump bids as natural, not ace-asking, when there is no sign of a suit fit.

7. *Are you planning to play in a minor suit?* If so, make sure you are not getting out of your depth. If your partner's response tells you that two aces are missing, but takes you beyond five of your trump suit, you are in trouble.

8. *Do you know what to do when your partner responds to Blackwood?* If you have to think on the next round, you were probably wrong to make the bid in the first place.

Even when Blackwood is used properly, there may be problems:

1. *What does the responder reply when he has four aces?* Five clubs, exactly as if he had no ace, and

his partner works it out from the previous bidding—though it will seldom happen that a player will bid four notrump without at least one ace.

2. *What does the responder do with a void?* He cannot regard a void as an ace, for this may lead to disaster—a slam immediately defeated by one or two opposing aces (exactly what Blackwood was designed to prevent). This is a partnership matter, and there are several theories. The following is recommended: bid five notrump with two aces and a void; with one ace and a void, bid the void suit at the six-level if it ranks below the trump suit (otherwise, bid six of the trump suit); with no ace and a void, bid just five clubs, for your hand may be worthless in controls.

3. *What do you do if the opponents bid over four notrump?* Again, there are several opinions. A method which is good and simple is to double with no ace or two aces, and to pass with one ace or three aces. This is called DOPI (that is: double with zero, pass with one).

4. *Can the responder go on to a small slam if the Blackwood bidder chooses to stop at the five level?* Decidedly not. The bidding has shown that there are two aces missing, so responder had better resist all temptation to bid on.

5. *Can the responder ever bid a grand slam?* Possibly. If the Blackwood bidder continues with five notrump, asking for kings, he guarantees that all four aces are held by the partnership. So with some hands the responder may be able to contract for seven.

BLACKWOOD QUIZ

In which of the following sequences is the four-notrump bid Blackwood?

1.
SOUTH	NORTH
1 ♡	4 ♡
4 NT	

2.
SOUTH	NORTH
1 NT	4 NT

3.
SOUTH	NORTH
1 NT	3 ♡
3 NT	4 NT

4.
SOUTH	NORTH
2 NT	4 NT

5.
SOUTH	NORTH
4 NT	

6.
SOUTH	NORTH
1 ♠	2 ♢
3 NT	4 ♣
4 NT	

7.
SOUTH	NORTH
2 ♠	3 NT
(strong two-bid)	
4 NT	

8.
SOUTH	NORTH
1 ♠	2 NT
3 ♢	3 NT
4 NT	

9.
SOUTH	NORTH
3 ♢	4 NT

10.
NORTH	EAST	SOUTH	WEST
3 ♡	4 ♡	Pass	4 NT

What would you bid as South in each of the given situations below?

11.
YOUR HAND:
♠ 5 3
♡ A Q 8 7 4
♢ 8
♣ K Q 9 6 3

NORTH	SOUTH
1 ♠	2 ♡
4 ♡	?

12. YOUR HAND:

		NORTH	SOUTH
♠	K 5	1 ♠	2 ♡
♡	A J 8 7 3	4 ♡	?
♢	Q 2		
♣	K Q 9 2		

13. YOUR HAND:

		SOUTH	WEST	NORTH	EAST
♠	A J 8 7 3 2	1 ♠	2 ♡	4 ♠	Pass
♡	7 5	?			
♢	A				
♣	A K 8 3				

14. YOUR HAND:

		SOUTH	NORTH
♠	A Q J 10 8 7 2	2 ♠	3 ♠
♡	A 9 3	4 ♠	4 NT
♢	A 5	?	
♣	A		

15. YOUR HAND:

		NORTH	EAST	SOUTH	WEST
♠	A 4 2	2 ♠	Pass	3 ♠	4 ♡
♡	9 6	4 NT	5 ♡	?	
♢	K 7 3 2				
♣	Q 6 5 3				

16. YOUR HAND:

		EAST	SOUTH	WEST	NORTH
♠	–	1 ♠	2 ♡	2 ♠	4 NT
♡	A Q 10 8 7 3	Pass	?		
♢	9 6 2				
♣	K Q 8 4				

ANSWERS TO BLACKWOOD QUIZ

1. *Blackwood.* A clear case, with agreement to play in a heart contract.

2. *Not Blackwood*. Another clear case. When no suit has been bid, four notrump is a natural invitation to bid six notrump.

3. *Blackwood*. The responder has an unbalanced hand, and is checking aces on the way to slam.

4. *Not Blackwood*. No suit has been bid.

5. *Not Blackwood*. A natural bid showing a balanced hand with about 27–28 high-card points. But this is not a very useful bid, and could be Blackwood by partnership agreement.

6. *Not Blackwood*. A player who was willing to play in three notrump, and has therefore limited his hand, cannot ask for aces. Four notrump here shows lack of interest in a slam and a desire to play four notrump.

7. *Blackwood*. The opening two-spade bidder can be assumed to have an unbalanced hand, and can hardly be interested in inviting a notrump slam. His hand is unlimited in strength.

8. *Blackwood*. The opening bidder has an unbalanced hand, and his strength is unlimited.

9. *Blackwood*. An unlikely bid, but the only conceivable interpretation is that it asks for aces.

10. *Not Blackwood*. East has shown a hand of enormous power and asked West to pick a suit. A very weak hand cannot normally invoke Blackwood opposite a very strong one, and four notrump is a natural bid, suggesting a final contract.

11. *Four notrump, Blackwood*. With your partner's strong bidding, there should be slam here if there is not more than one ace missing. You have some control in the two unbid suits, and you do not

need to worry about spades, which your partner has bid.

12. *Five clubs.* Your hand is too strong to abandon slam hopes, but Blackwood would be a mistake. If your partner showed two aces you would have to bid a slam, and the opponents might take the ace-king of diamonds. (Whenever you bid Blackwood you should be ready to bid a slam if your side has at least three aces.) Five clubs shows some control in that suit and invites six hearts. Your partner may jump to six hearts or make a cue bid of five diamonds, which is what you want to hear. If he signs off in five hearts, you pass— because he is denying diamond control.

13. *Five spades.* Again, Blackwood is a bad move with two quick losers in one suit. The natural invitation of five spades implies control of the unbid suits and asks partner to go on if he has first- or second-round control of the opponents' heart suit.

14. *Five clubs.* The conventional reply in this very rare situation in which the responder to Blackwood has all four aces. The bidding will always enable the Blackwood bidder to determine whether five clubs means zero or four aces and more bidding space is available for a grand slam exploration.

15. *Pass.* Showing one ace according to the DOPI method. But other agreements are possible. Some partnerships would bid five spades to show one ace.

16. *Six Hearts.* Showing one ace and a void in a higher-ranking suit according to the method sug-

gested above. Some partnerships bid six diamonds to show one ace and a void (because five diamonds would show one ace), but this is less precise.

Experts do not rely on Blackwood to the same degree as lesser players. They cue-bid more to seek out makeable slams. But let's look in again on their habits:

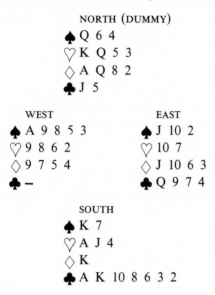

NORTH (DUMMY)
♠ Q 6 4
♡ K Q 5 3
♢ A Q 8 2
♣ J 5

WEST
♠ A 9 8 5 3
♡ 9 8 6 2
♢ 9 7 5 4
♣ —

EAST
♠ J 10 2
♡ 10 7
♢ J 10 6 3
♣ Q 9 7 4

SOUTH
♠ K 7
♡ A J 4
♢ K
♣ A K 10 8 6 3 2

Both sides vulnerable.

NORTH	EAST	SOUTH	WEST
1 ♢	Pass	3 ♣	Pass
3 NT	Pass	4 NT	Pass
5 ♢	Pass	6 ♣	All pass

A player who intends to play in a club contract needs two aces to use Blackwood since a five-diamond response puts him in slam anyway. The South hand qualified in this deal, and as he had already shown slam ambitions by jumping to three clubs there was no danger that the bid would be interpreted as a natural slam invitation. Notice that South was not afraid of losing two quick tricks in either of the unbid major suits.

West led the spade ace. (With any other lead, South would have been able to discard both his spades on dummy's diamonds.) Declarer won the spade continuation with the king and carefully entered dummy by overtaking the diamond king with the ace.

He continued with the club jack, and East fell into the trap by covering with the queen. This seems a natural play—holding the club nine as a possible trick —but it was disastrous. South won with the king and West showed out. It was now a simple matter to enter dummy for a marked trump finesse to bring home the slam.

If East had played low quickly, the declarer would no doubt have misguessed and played the king from his hand. There were two small clues for East. South's powerful bidding was a little more likely to be based on a 7-card suit than a 6-card suit; and the declarer would probably have led low from dummy if he had been missing five trumps, to guard against a singleton queen in the East hand.

However, if East had stopped to think this out he would have betrayed his possession of the club queen. It was necessary to have done the thinking in advance, before the club jack was led from the dummy, and that would have required remarkable alertness.

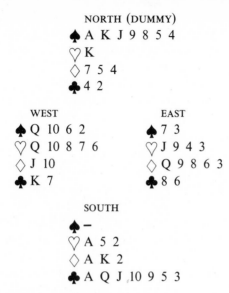

NORTH (DUMMY)
♠ A K J 9 8 5 4
♡ K
◇ 7 5 4
♣ 4 2

WEST
♠ Q 10 6 2
♡ Q 10 8 7 6
◇ J 10
♣ K 7

EAST
♠ 7 3
♡ J 9 4 3
◇ Q 9 8 6 3
♣ 8 6

SOUTH
♠ —
♡ A 5 2
◇ A K 2
♣ A Q J 10 9 5 3

East-West vulnerable.

NORTH	EAST	SOUTH	WEST
1 ♠	Pass	3 ♣	Pass
4 ♠	Pass	4 NT	Pass
5 ◇	Pass	5 NT	Pass
6 ♡	Pass	6 NT	All Pass

To use Blackwood when holding a void suit is usually a mistake, because a response that shows that two aces are missing creates a problem. The Blackwood bidder will not know whether or not his side has two quick losers.

An exception arises, as here, when the four-notrump bidder has three aces in his hand and intends to continue to a small slam in any event. In that case Blackwood is simply an exploration toward a grand slam. Six clubs would obviously have been safe, but this was a match-point game and South wanted the extra points available in notrump.

The five-notrump bid not only asked for kings, but indicated that the partnership held all four aces. North would have continued to the grand slam if he had held the club king instead of the heart king.

South won the diamond lead with the ace and counted twelve potential tricks: six clubs and two in each of the other suits. Taking them safely was less easy.

If South had taken his three tricks in dummy and finessed in clubs, West would have made two immediate tricks to defeat the slam. Playing the ace and queen of clubs immediately would have been no more successful, for West might then have led a second round of diamonds, cutting South's communications. There would have been no way to cash the spade winners and return to the closed hand.

South made his best play by leading the club queen immediately. West won with the king, and South claimed his contract. Whatever the return from West, there would still be a minor-suit entry to the closed hand.

South was lucky that the club king was played on his queen, for otherwise he would have to guess whether the king was now singleton or East had K-x remaining—the two holdings that can bring in the slam.

He was even luckier he didn't get the opening lead of a heart, which would destroy his communications and surely put him down.

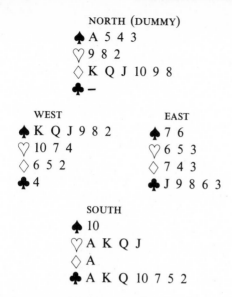

NORTH (DUMMY)
♠ A 5 4 3
♡ 9 8 2
◇ K Q J 10 9 8
♣ —

WEST
♠ K Q J 9 8 2
♡ 10 7 4
◇ 6 5 2
♣ 4

EAST
♠ 7 6
♡ 6 5 3
◇ 7 4 3
♣ J 9 8 6 3

SOUTH
♠ 10
♡ A K Q J
◇ A
♣ A K Q 10 7 5 2

East-West vulnerable.

SOUTH	WEST	NORTH	EAST
2 ♣	Pass	3 ◇	Pass
4 ♣	Pass	4 ♠	Pass
4 NT	Pass	5 ◇	Pass
6 ♣	Pass	6 NT	All pass

The Blackwood bidder is normally in control, and his partner, in principle, is barred from taking the initiative. But the responder may be entitled to attempt a grand slam if the Blackwood bidder has asked for kings with five notrump, thereby indicating that the partnership has all the aces. And, in rare circumstances, the responder may decide to move from one small slam to another.

North was right to move on the deal shown, but he moved in the wrong direction. All thirteen tricks could have been made in diamonds, but South had a problem at six notrump.

South prepared for the possibility that the club jack would not drop, and set a trap for West. He allowed the opening lead of the spade king to win, a most unusual play for a man with a singleton spade and no entry to the dummy.

South hoped for a spade continuation, which he could win in dummy while unblocking the diamond ace from his hand. This would enable him to cash enough diamonds to take care of his losing clubs.

But West worked out the motive behind the duck, and shifted to a diamond, a killing defense. South squirmed, glowered, and went down ungraciously. West looked smug, East looked happy, and then came the post-mortem.

South cursed his partner for bidding six notrump instead of six diamonds, and North cursed back at South for failing to bid five notrump, a king-asking bid which would have allowed North to bid seven diamonds.

East and West said nothing.

OVERBIDDING STRONG HANDS AND UNDERBIDDING WEAK ONES

The great majority of inexperienced players overbid with powerful hands and underbid with weak hands. Suppose you are South, holding:

♠ A Q 8 3   ♡ A K J 2   ◇ K Q 4   ♣ 9 2

East bids one club, and you double. North responds one spade, with the opponents now silent. What do you bid?

Many players would jump to four spades, hoping that partner has a hand of modest strength, not a yarborough. The contract will often be made, but this does not excuse the overbid.

A jump to three spades is quite sufficient opposite a partner who has been forced to bid and may have nothing. (The doubler's 19 high-card points will not produce a game by themselves; even a nine-trick contract may not be safe, but some risks must be run.)

Now suppose you are *North* with the same bidding and hold:

♠ K 10 7 6 2   ♡ Q 5 3   ◇ 9 8 6   ♣ 10 6

This began as a very bad hand, but it has improved in the light of the bidding. South's jump to three spades has strongly invited game; you have a 5-card trump suit, a valuable king, and an important queen. You should bid four spades and might even do so without the heart queen.

Yet, most players regularly bid four spades with the South hand and, if they get the chance, pass the North hand out at three spades. When they do get to the proper contract, it is blind luck guiding them. Yet, a player with a very weak hand should often bid aggressively in the later stages of the auction because he can judge that his meager strength will fit his partner's hand. As in this case.

62 PRACTICAL BRIDGE

There is a simple rule which will prevent most underbidding and overbidding. Ask yourself this question: "Have I got more strength than my previous
bidding promised?"

If the answer is "yes," you can afford to bid with
some vigor, although you must of course avoid taking
the bidding to an unsafe level. If the answer is "no,"
make a discouraging bid and pass at the earliest convenient moment.

Do not say to yourself "I have a great hand," but
rather "Is it greater than my partner expects?" Do not
say "I have a terrible hand," but rather "Is it quite as
bad as my partner thinks?"

Consider the following hands:

WEST	EAST (a)	EAST (b)
♠ A Q J 10 9 5	♠ 6 2	♠ K 2
♡ A Q J 10 8 3	♡ 7 5 2	♡ K 5
◇ A	◇ K J 5 3	◇ 9 8 7 4 3
♣ –	♣ Q 10 7 5	♣ 8 6 4 3

Most West players would drive to a slam with no
encouragement from East, and would feel aggrieved
when they lost two tricks opposite hand (a). "Bad luck,
partner," they will complain in the post-mortem. "If
only your king had been in one of my suits."

And most East players would let West play at a
game contract with hand (b) if given the chance. "I
couldn't do anything with my terrible hand," they'd
announce afterwards. "I only had six points."

And they would both be quite wrong.

There must be some way to stop short of slam with

East hand (a) and to reach a grand slam with East hand (b). And there is.

When East holds hand (a) above, the bidding should go:

WEST	EAST
2 ♠	2 NT
3 ♡	3 NT
5 ♡	Pass

West jumps to five hearts at his third turn to show that his hand alone will produce eleven tricks. But East declines to bid the slam, for he has no help in either of West's suits.

When East holds hand (b) above, the bidding should go:

WEST	EAST
2 ♠	2 NT
3 ♡	3 ♠
5 ♡	7 ♡ or 7 ♠
Pass	

West shows a game-going hand, and East responds negatively. When West shows his second suit, East simply gives a preference to three spades. And now West bids five hearts, in the face of persistent discouragement.

East should realize that he can certainly contribute two tricks to the cause. West must be expecting to lose tricks to the two major-suit kings, and East can plug both those gaps. So he can bid the grand slam with confidence. It does not matter much which grand slam he bids, but an expert would bid seven hearts to leave

West the choice. If West is missing the jack of one of his suits he will have a slight advantage in playing in his stronger suit.

This shows both sides of the coin. The strong hand does not necessarily have to gamble: if he describes his power and distribution, he can sometimes leave his partner to take over. And the weak hand can sometimes make crucial decisions by judging whether the little strength he has will prove useful to his partner.

Temptations to overbid and underbid will be present in the following quiz. Resist them.

OVERBIDDING AND UNDERBIDDING QUIZ

Unless otherwise stated, neither side is vulnerable. You sit South in each case. What do you bid?

	YOUR HAND:	SOUTH	WEST	NORTH	EAST
1.	♠ K 5	1 ♣	Pass	1 ♡	Pass
	♡ A Q 8 2	?			
	◇ Q 6				
	♣ K Q J 7 2				

	YOUR HAND:	SOUTH	WEST	NORTH	EAST
2.	♠ A Q J 7 2	2 ♠	Pass	3 ♠	Pass
	♡ K 6 2	?			
	◇ A K 5				
	♣ A Q				

	YOUR HAND:	NORTH	EAST	SOUTH	WEST
3.	♠ A K 4	Pass	Pass	1 ♣	Pass
	♡ Q J 5	2 NT	Pass	?	
	◇ K 9 2				
	♣ A Q J 5				

4. YOUR HAND:

	SOUTH	WEST	NORTH	EAST
♠ K 5	1 ♣	Pass	1 ♡	2 ♠
♡ A Q 8 2	?			(pre-
◇ Q 6				emptive)
♣ K Q J 7 2				

5. YOUR HAND:

	EAST	SOUTH	WEST	NORTH
♠ K 8 7 3	1 ♣	Dbl.	Pass	2 ♠
♡ A Q 7 4	Pass	?		
◇ K 6 3				
♣ Q 9				

6. YOUR HAND:

	NORTH	EAST	SOUTH	WEST
♠ K 7 4 2	1 ♠	Dbl.	?	
♡ 4				
◇ K 9 6 3				
♣ J 8 4 2				

7. YOUR HAND:

	NORTH	EAST	SOUTH	WEST
♠ K J 4	1 ♣	1 ♡	Pass	Pass
♡ 8 5 3 2	2 ♠	Pass	?	
◇ 10 7 6 2				
♣ 4 2				

8. YOUR HAND:

	NORTH	EAST	SOUTH	WEST
♠ 6	3 ♠	Pass	?	
♡ K Q 9 2				
◇ Q J 5 2				
♣ A K 6 3				

9. YOUR HAND:

	NORTH	EAST	SOUTH	WEST
♠ 7 4	2 ♠	Pass	2 NT	Pass
♡ K J 6 2	3 ♡	Pass	?	
◇ 10 7 6 4 3 2				
♣ 5				

10. YOUR HAND:

	WEST	NORTH	EAST	SOUTH
♠ K 9 6 2	3 ◇	Dbl.	Pass	?
♡ A 10 9 6 3				
◇ 8 7 2				
♣ 9				

11. YOUR HAND:

	NORTH	EAST	SOUTH	WEST
♠ 6 5	2 ♠	Pass	2 NT	Pass
♡ A 6 2	6 ♡	Pass	?	
◇ 10 7 6 4 3				
♣ 9 8 3				

ANSWERS TO OVERBIDDING AND UNDERBIDDING QUIZ

1. *Three hearts.* If North has a minimum response, there is unlikely to be a sound play for game. North has promised 6 points, and if he has anything in reserve, he will continue. Remember that a jump by the opener in a suit already bid is invitational, not forcing.

2. *Three notrump* (or four spades). This was a borderline two-bid in the first place, and some players would prefer a two notrump opening. Even when there is a positive response, South should bid three notrump, putting on the brakes. Any slam move can be left to North, who knows the situation. If he has a minimum positive response—perhaps an ace, a king, and a jack, for example—he will be content to play in game. A positive response to a two-bid usually leads to a slam, but this hand may be one of the exceptions.

3. *Three notrump.* Remember that North passed

originally and cannot have 13 points. He probably has 11 or 12 points, and the combined total of 31 or 32 points is not sufficient to make six notrump. There is no reason to go beyond game unless there is a real prospect of a slam.

4. *Four hearts.* The same hand as 1. above, but a more ambitious bid for two reasons. The spade king is a probable trick once the spades have been bid to the right, and South has to bid "under pressure." He might be forced to bid three hearts with a rather weaker hand because the two-spade bid has barred a two-heart raise. North will allow for this pressure and pass three hearts with a hand which would otherwise call for a game bid.

5. *Pass.* The jump response to a takeout double is encouraging but not forcing. If North wishes to insist on a game, he must make a cue bid of two clubs. The club queen is likely to be valueless, so South had a minimum double. With nothing in reserve, pass at the first sensible opportunity. If South held the spade or diamond queen instead of the club queen, he could raise to three spades.

6. *Three spades.* A situation in which overbidding is called for. This hand would be worth just two spades without the intervening double, but there is good reason to try to shut out the opponents who probably have a fit in the heart suit. The opening bidder should be aware that his partner is "stretching" in such circumstances.

7. *Four spades.* Not a timid three spades, which partner might pass. Your bad hand has suddenly

become a very good one. The opener has shown at least five clubs, at least five spades, and a hand not far short of a two-bid. He will be able to establish his clubs by ruffing in the dummy, and ten tricks should be made easily. The king-jack of spades are "golden cards." Whenever partner shows a strong two-suiter, honors in his suits become worth their weight in gold, and low honors in other suits are almost certainly useless.

8. *Pass.* 15 high-card points will not be enough for game opposite a three-spade opening bid. North can be expected to have a broken 7-card suit with hardly any outside strength. Even if his suit is as strong as A–Q–J–x–x–x–x, there are likely to be four losers at a spade contract. Three notrump would be a dreadful bid, for there will be no side-suit entry to the spades even if they can be established.

9. *Four clubs.* A bad hand has improved considerably, and a mere raise to four hearts would neglect definite slam prospects. A jump to five hearts has merit, but an advance cue bid of four clubs followed by a bid of five hearts is better. This will show heart support and some club control, which will help North to bid the slam if he is concerned about his club losers.

10. *Four diamonds.* North's double is for takeout, and there is surely a good fit in one or both of the major suits. South's hand is very suitable for game, because his partner will surely ruff diamonds and South can ruff club losers. It would be cowardly to bid three hearts, the same bid that shows a

yarborough. Four hearts would be an acceptable bid, but four diamonds is even better. This cue bid simply asks North to bid a major suit.

11. *Seven hearts.* North has guaranteed that he can make a small slam opposite a yarborough. He must be expecting to lose a heart trick, so with the heart ace in dummy, he can surely make a grand slam. Notice that South should not bid seven on the strength of a minor-suit ace in such a position: North might be void in that suit and have an unavoidable loser elsewhere.

For a change of pace, let's look at the effect of an expert's deliberate overbid:

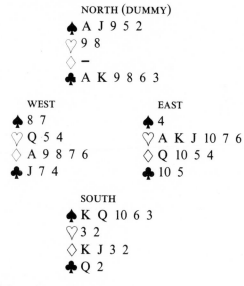

```
                NORTH (DUMMY)
                ♠ A J 9 5 2
                ♡ 9 8
                ◇ —
                ♣ A K 9 8 6 3

    WEST                      EAST
    ♠ 8 7                     ♠ 4
    ♡ Q 5 4                   ♡ A K J 10 7 6
    ◇ A 9 8 7 6               ◇ Q 10 5 4
    ♣ J 7 4                   ♣ 10 5

                SOUTH
                ♠ K Q 10 6 3
                ♡ 3 2
                ◇ K J 3 2
                ♣ Q 2
```

Neither side vulnerable.

SOUTH	WEST	NORTH	EAST
Pass	Pass	1 ♣	4 ♡
4 ♠	5 ♡	7 ♠	All pass
Pass	Pass		

Here's a case of a carefully calculated overbid, not a careless one. Such a tactical stroke may earn a handsome reward when the hand is freakish and both sides are bidding. North electrified everyone at the table by jumping to a grand slam in spades at his second turn. Ironically, he could not have made six spades if he bid it, but he did bid and make seven spades.

Any slam was likely to depend on the opening lead, for there was a danger of losing two immediate heart tricks. North correctly diagnosed this as a "five or seven" hand, one that will make eleven tricks or thirteen tricks, but never exactly twelve.

On the reasonable assumption that his side had no black-suit losers, North jumped to the grand slam. If he could bluff West out of leading a heart he would gain a grand slam bonus of 1000 points, whereas his potential loss was a non-vulnerable game worth about 450 points.

It was certainly difficult for West to imagine that the grand-slam bidder was wide open in the heart suit. In the belief that North held either the heart ace or a void, West naturally led his diamond ace, and the play was easy for South. He simply ruffed in dummy, drew trumps, discarded his heart losers on dummy's club winners, and had a bridge story he would tell for years.

More often, an overbid leads to a minus result, as on this hand:

NORTH (DUMMY)
♠ J 9 8 6 4
♡ 8 7 3
◇ A 5
♣ 7 6 2

WEST
♠ K Q 7 3
♡ 5 2
◇ Q J 9 7
♣ K Q J

EAST
♠ 10 5 2
♡ 6 4
◇ 6 4 3 2
♣ 9 8 5 4

SOUTH
♠ A
♡ A K Q J 10 9
◇ K 10 8
♣ A 10 3

Both sides vulnerable.

SOUTH	WEST	NORTH	EAST
2 ♡	Pass	2 NT	Pass
3 ♡	Pass	4 ♡	Pass
4 NT	Pass	5 ◇	Pass
6 NT	All pass		

South had his values for his forcing bid of two hearts, but he had nothing in reserve and should have subsided in four hearts. Conversely, North underbid slightly at his second turn; having made a negative response, he was justified in bidding five hearts now (or four diamonds followed by five hearts) for South had no reason to place him with an ace, a doubleton, and three trumps.

Often one player's overbid is offset by his partner's

underbid, and a sound contract is reached with no one the wiser. But this was not one of those hands.

South was lucky to find the dummy with a doubleton diamond, but he still had two club losers in six hearts. Ironically, South's trumps were too good. If the ten-nine of hearts had been in the dummy instead of the eight-seven, South would have had sufficient entries to establish and use dummy's fifth spade.

Even as it was, the defenders had to be careful. West led the club king; South held up his ace on the first trick and West led a second club. South won and led three rounds of diamonds for a ruff in dummy. Six rounds of trumps followed, and West could tell that South was left with the spade ace and one other card. Obviously this was not a diamond, which would have been ruffed in dummy.

West defeated the contract by carefully watching his partner's discards. East had thrown his two remaining clubs, followed by his last diamond, thus showing that he had no more clubs. In such circumstances, a player whose cards are worthless should usually get rid of one entire suit first. When he discards a new suit, his partner is able to tell he is out of the first and can count the hand. It would have been bad defense for East to shift discards aimlessly from suit to suit like a nervous butterfly.

With East's informative discarding, however, West could count declarer's last card for a club. So he kept his club honor. This not only set the slam but gave South good reason to reflect on the folly of bidding the same values twice.

For our last exhibit, a brilliant underbid:

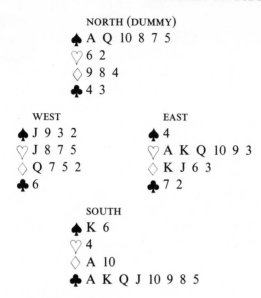

NORTH (DUMMY)
♠ A Q 10 8 7 5
♡ 6 2
◇ 9 8 4
♣ 4 3

WEST
♠ J 9 3 2
♡ J 8 7 5
◇ Q 7 5 2
♣ 6

EAST
♠ 4
♡ A K Q 10 9 3
◇ K J 6 3
♣ 7 2

SOUTH
♠ K 6
♡ 4
◇ A 10
♣ A K Q J 10 9 8 5

North-South vulnerable.

NORTH	EAST	SOUTH	WEST
Pass	1 ♡	2 ♣	2 ♡
2 ♠	4 ♡	5 ♣	Pass
Pass	5 ♡	6 ♣	All pass

Tactical underbidding may be indicated with a freak hand such as South's. The important thing in such cases is to make sure that you become the declarer; the level at which you play the hand is of secondary importance. If you underbid initially, persistent bidding later will sound like optimism or a sacrifice.

The overcall of two clubs on this deal was just such a tactical underbid. South was sure that the bidding would continue, and he wished to disguise the strength of his hand. When North then bid two spades, showing a good suit, South could see prospects of making twelve tricks.

Nevertheless, he continued his tactics by bidding only five clubs over East's four hearts. A confident jump to six clubs would surely have provoked the opponents into sacrificing. As it was, the eventual six-club bid sounded as though South was bidding one more "for luck," which is often a good policy with a distributional hand.

East gave South a suspicious look, but finally gave up, and the contract was easy to make. Six hearts doubled would have been down two, an economical save for East-West.

DANGEROUS OVERCALLS

Most inexperienced players overcall too often, perhaps because they think of overcalling in the same light as an opening bid. Suppose both sides are vulnerable and your right-hand opponent bids one heart. You have:

♠ K 7 4 3
♡ A Q 3 2
♢ 9
♣ K Q 6 2

What do you bid?

One spade? Two clubs? One notrump? Double? All of these are unwise, for a variety of reasons.

One spade would promise a 5-card suit, for an overcall with only four cards is generally pointless as well as risky. The same objection applies more strongly to two clubs, because this takes the bidding to a higher level.

A takeout double of one heart would promise some support for all unbid suits. In this case you are not prepared for a response of two diamonds. This would no doubt be a foolish contract, and any further bid by you would suggest a stronger hand. Finally, one no-trump would show the equivalent of a notrump opening bid, 16–18 points and a balanced hand.

The answer, of course, is that you should pass the opening bid of one heart. This would provoke a protest from some players: "But I have a good opening bid; I must do something."

However, the rules for opening the bidding have no validity once the opponents have gotten in the first blow. Now there are several different considerations, and the overall point count is only one factor:

1. *What is the trick potential?* The overcaller needs some insurance against disaster. Unlike the opening bidder he may be quickly doubled for penalties, since his left-hand opponent can count on the strength of the opening bid.

   The best insurance is a 5-card suit with some internal solidity, or a 6-card suit.

   (a) ♠ K J 10 8 5   (b) ♠ J 9 6 3 2

   Suit (a), above, is an acceptable suit for an overcall if the other factors are right. But it will hardly ever be right to overcall with suit (b). With such a weak holding there is a danger of being doubled, and no advantage in suggesting a productive lead to partner.

2. *Who is vulnerable?* This is a factor that should not concern the opening bidder, but it is of great importance to the overcaller. If he is vulnerable he must be more cautious. The opponents' vulnerability is also significant. A player who is not vulnerable against vulnerable opponents can make bids that might seem frivolous. Conversely, a player who is vulnerable against non-vulnerable should carry timidity to extremes.

   To deprive the opponents of a vulnerable game it pays to go down 500 points, which means three tricks if your side is not vulnerable. But to save a non-vulnerable game you should not be willing to pay more than 300 points, so down one doubled (200) should be the limit if you are vulnerable.

3. *At what level can an overcall be made?* At the one-level, the overcaller has considerable safety. The opposition can rarely impose a damaging penalty. When they can, they may not appreciate this possibility in time.

   But a good player is more likely to double at the two-level and exact a stinging penalty. And at higher levels the jeopardy increases.

4. *Will the overcall lead anywhere?* An overcall in spades is always tempting. There is a fair chance of outbidding the opponents if a spade fit can be discovered. Perhaps you can make a part score, or push the opponents out of their depth, or uncover a cheap save in four spades over four hearts. Overcalling in hearts also has some attractions. But overcalls in the minor suits seldom lead anywhere.

5. *Is the hand strong enough?* For most purposes the overcaller should have enough high-card strength to open the bidding. But he can lower his standards if he has an eye on a possible sacrifice, which usually means that he must be not vulnerable against vulnerable opponents.

These considerations apply to the simple overcall in a suit when an opponent has opened with one of a suit. If the opposing opening bid was one notrump, or if both opponents have bid, greater caution must be exercised. The chance that your side can make a game has been reduced, so it is foolhardy to expose yourself to a double with little potential profit. An overcall in such cases usually indicates a 6-card suit.

Perhaps the whole matter can be summarized in one final question:

6. *Do circumstances favor attack or defense?* Circumstances favoring attack are: a long suit, or, better, two long suits; strength in the long suit; being non-vulnerable; high cards in long suits, not in short suits; a good spade suit.

   Circumstances favoring defense are: balanced distribution; length or strength in the opponent's suit; being vulnerable; having high cards in short suits.

Careful attention to these points should allow you to score well in the quiz which follows.

OVERCALL QUIZ

1. East is dealer and both sides are vulnerable. You are South and hold:

♠ K 6 3   ♡ A Q 7 6 2   ◇ Q J 4   ♣ J 7

What action would you take if East bids:
(a) one club?
(b) one diamond?
(c) one heart?
(d) one spade?

2. You have the same hand, and the vulnerability is the same, but West deals and bids one club. What do you do after North passes and East responds:
(a) one diamond?
(b) one spade?

3. Would any of your answers to (1) and (2) change if your side was not vulnerable?

4. Neither side is vulnerable. West deals and bids one spade. North overcalls with two clubs. Which of the following hands is he more likely to have?

(a) ♠ K J 4
   ♡ Q 5
   ◇ 6 5 2
   ♣ A K 7 5 3

(c) ♠ 6
   ♡ A J 4
   ◇ 10 5 3
   ♣ A J 7 6 4 2

(b) ♠ A J 4
   ♡ 6
   ◇ 10 5 3
   ♣ A J 7 5 4 2

(d) ♠ 4
   ♡ 5 3
   ◇ Q 7 2
   ♣ A K J 10 7 5 3

ANSWERS TO OVERCALL QUIZ

1. (a) *Bid one heart.* You have a fair 5-card suit and the strength for an opening bid. Your side may be able to make a heart contract, and the risk of being doubled is slight.

(b) *Bid one heart.* For the same reasons, but slightly more reluctantly. The possession of three diamonds including two honors gives the hand a slightly stronger defensive slant.

(c) *Pass.* Without any hesitation. Whenever the opponents bid a suit you were about to bid, simply pass. The hand is likely to be a misfit, and the side that plays it may be in trouble.

(d) *Pass.* To overcall vulnerable at the two level would be much too dangerous. A double could easily result in a penalty of 800 or 1100, and the chance that your side can make a game is slight. A vulnerable overcall at the level of two usually requires a 6-card suit, or perhaps a very strong 5-card suit.

2. (a) *Pass.* There is some temptation to bid, but it is easy to run into trouble when each opponent has bid his suit and partner is silent.

(b) *Pass.* Now there is no temptation, for action would have to be at the two-level.

3. *None of these answers* would change if you are not vulnerable, but 1 (d) and 2 (a) become close decisions and an overcall would not be completely out of line.

4. *Hand (c)* would be the most suitable one for an overcall of two clubs. It has a 6-card suit which is desirable for action at the two-level, and if partner has club support, a save in five clubs over four spades may be desirable.

Hand (b) would also be an acceptable overcall, but has a disadvantage. As the ace-jack of spades probably represent two spade tricks in defense, there is some danger that the two-club overcall might push partner into a phantom save—bidding five clubs and conceding a penalty when four spades would fail.

Hand (a) would be a dreadful overcall of two clubs, as it has considerable defensive strength and will not be good in attack. The suit is too poor to justify action at the two-level.

Hand (d) would be an inappropriate overcall of two clubs for a different reason. With a long, strong suit and little outside strength, pre-emptive action is called for. A jump to four clubs would be about right, although some would go all the way to five clubs, and others—who use a jump overcall as a weak bid—would be content with three clubs.

Now let's kibitz some experts' overcalls:

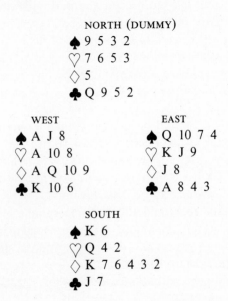

NORTH (DUMMY)
♠ 9 5 3 2
♡ 7 6 5 3
♢ 5
♣ Q 9 5 2

WEST
♠ A J 8
♡ A 10 8
♢ A Q 10 9
♣ K 10 6

EAST
♠ Q 10 7 4
♡ K J 9
♢ J 8
♣ A 8 4 3

SOUTH
♠ K 6
♡ Q 4 2
♢ K 7 6 4 3 2
♣ J 7

East-West vulnerable.

WEST	NORTH	EAST	SOUTH
1 ♣	Pass	2 ♣	3 ◇
Dbl.	All pass		

This deal was played in the 1958 World Championship in Como, Italy, and East and West were playing a conventional system in which one club was strong and forcing. The response of two clubs conventionally showed an ace and a king or three kings.

South believed that his opponents were on the way to a slam, and thought he could take advantage of the favorable vulnerability to make a pre-emptive jump overcall. As the sequel showed, this was indiscreet for two reasons: The diamond suit was not good enough for pre-emptive action when the opponents had already exchanged information about their strength; and South had too much strength outside diamonds.

West naturally doubled three diamonds, and an opening club lead followed by careful defense held South to two tricks. He lost two spades, two clubs, three hearts, and four trumps.

The loss thus amounted to 1300 points. It would not have been a disaster if East-West had been able to bid and make a slam. Six notrump could be made with a degree of luck, but East-West were unlikely to get there with a combined point count of 29 points and no long suit.

When the Americans held the East West cards they were, quite rightly, content to play three notrump, and made an overtrick, worth a total of 630. So the net American loss was 670 points.

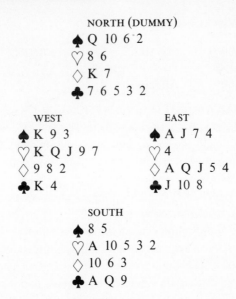

NORTH (DUMMY)
♠ Q 10 6 2
♡ 8 6
◇ K 7
♣ 7 6 5 3 2

WEST
♠ K 9 3
♡ K Q J 9 7
◇ 9 8 2
♣ K 4

EAST
♠ A J 7 4
♡ 4
◇ A Q J 5 4
♣ J 10 8

SOUTH
♠ 8 5
♡ A 10 5 3 2
◇ 10 6 3
♣ A Q 9

North-South vulnerable.

EAST	SOUTH	WEST	NORTH
1 ◇	1 ♡	Dbl.	All pass

South made an unsound overcall on this deal. His suit was rather feeble, and did not have the strength needed for a vulnerable overcall. One heart doubled was a disaster. West led the diamond nine and East captured dummy's king with the ace. He shifted to a trump, and South ducked. West won with the heart nine, and led the heart king.

South took this, and was in a hopeless position. He led a spade hoping eventually to make two club tricks, but West put up the spade king, cashed the heart queen, and shifted back to diamonds.

South unwisely ruffed the fourth round of diamonds and West over-ruffed. The heart jack drew South's ten, and all the players were down to four cards. East had discarded all his clubs, and had three spades and a diamond. After a spade lead from West the defense took two spade tricks and a diamond trick, but dummy's spade queen took the last trick. The result was down five, a penalty of 1400, when the best East-West could have done if left to themselves was to bid three notrump and make game, worth about 400 points. Even if South had played the hand better, he could not have escaped a penalty of less than 1100 points.

On the following deal the overcaller escaped punishment, but the overcall helped the declarer in the play of the hand:

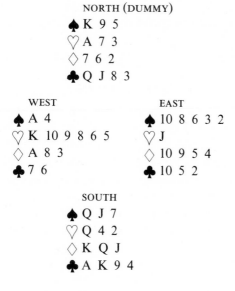

```
                NORTH (DUMMY)
                ♠ K 9 5
                ♡ A 7 3
                ◇ 7 6 2
                ♣ Q J 8 3

  WEST                          EAST
  ♠ A 4                         ♠ 10 8 6 3 2
  ♡ K 10 9 8 6 5                ♡ J
  ◇ A 8 3                       ◇ 10 9 5 4
  ♣ 7 6                         ♣ 10 5 2

                SOUTH
                ♠ Q J 7
                ♡ Q 4 2
                ◇ K Q J
                ♣ A K 9 4
```

Both sides vulnerable.

SOUTH	WEST	NORTH	EAST
1 NT	2 ♡	3 NT	All pass

South had an obvious opening bid of one notrump, and West had barely enough to overcall with two hearts. Bidding over one notrump is especially danger- ous, and the requirements are therefore more stringent than those for an overcall of a suit bid. An opening bid and a substantial 6-card suit is needed, a standard which West could just meet.

North knew that his side held enough points for a game, so he simply jumped to three notrump. He could have doubled instead and beaten West by two tricks— 500 points—with ordinary defense.

Against three notrump West led the heart ten. South played low from dummy and paused to consider when East played the jack. It was clear to him that West must have the two missing aces. And it was equally clear that East's heart jack was a singleton, for West would not overcall with five hearts headed by the king-ten.

With this inference South found the winning play. He permitted the heart jack to win. As he expected, East was unable to continue the suit and South remained one jump ahead. If West continued hearts when he gained the lead, both his aces would be forced out be- fore his hearts could be established. The best West could do was to play passively, leaving South with nine tricks —two spades, one heart, two diamonds, and four clubs.

West would have been in control of the situation if South had made the obvious play of capturing the heart jack with the queen at the first trick.

South's best chance would have been to lead the seven of spades at the second trick to try to steal a spade trick before switching to diamonds. But West hops up with his spade ace, continues hearts, and still has the diamond ace as entry to his now-established hearts.

In the post-mortem West discovered that he could have beaten the hand, despite South's fine play. If he had led the heart king—not an impossible play in the circumstances—he would have smothered his partner's jack but held the lead so that a hold up by South would not have saved the day.

MISJUDGING COMPETITIVE SITUATIONS

A bright beginner who studies the textbooks can bid nearly as well as an expert after a few months' experience—provided his opponents are obligingly silent.

But it will take him several years to develop good judgment in the multitude of situations in which both sides are bidding. The great majority of players, however enthusiastic, never graduate in this area.

There is no substitute here for experience and common sense, but we can draw your attention to a number of relevant points, other than the overcalling situations already described.

1. *Balancing.* Should you reopen the bidding if the opponents stop at a low level?

    Frequently yes.

    Your opponents, if they know their business, have less than 26 points between them. The odds are that both sides are somewhere in the 17–23 point range. It will be worthwhile to compete if you can make a part score instead of your opponents; or if you can push them up to a level where they will be defeated.

A balancing action—that is, a reopening bid when the opponents have stopped at a low level—may be made with as little as 10 points or even fewer. The opponents' bidding has told you that your partner has considerable high-card strength, so the normal requirements for overcalling and doubling do not apply. To some extent, you are bidding the high-card strength you can infer in your partner's hand, and he should be aware of this.

Balancing is indicated if either side seems to have a fit. Suppose the bidding proceeds:

SOUTH	WEST	NORTH	EAST
1 ◇	Pass	2 ◇	Pass
Pass	?		

And you hold as West:

♠ K J 4 3   ♡ A 10 7 3   ◇ 8 4 2   ♣ J 6

It is highly probable that East-West can make two spades or two hearts. West should almost always take some action, either bidding a major himself or doubling, as in this case, to invite his partner to do so.

Balancing is contra-indicated if it appears that the hand is a misfit. Suppose the bidding starts:

SOUTH	WEST	NORTH	EAST
1 ♠	Pass	Pass	?

East has:

♠ K J 4 3   ♡ 5   ◇ A Q 6 3   ♣ Q J 8 2

Although he has a full opening bid, East should pass one spade. His length and strength in spades suggests a misfit, and it pays to defend misfit hands. Also, the singleton heart is a danger signal. If West has a long heart suit East does not want him to bid it. And if not, North-South have a good fit in hearts, perhaps even a game, which they may discover if given a second chance.

Balancing against one notrump is usually wrong, for if your opponents cannot find a fit in a suit, the chances are that you will not either.

2. *Action by balancer's partner.* When your partner has balanced, be very cautious about bidding. Remember that he is already expecting you to have fair strength. Your side is fighting a battle for the part score, not looking for a game contract.

The bidding has been:

SOUTH	WEST	NORTH	EAST
1 ◇	Pass	2 ◇	Pass
Pass	Dbl.	Pass	?

You are East and hold:

♠ A Q 7 2   ♡ 9 6 2   ◇ J 6   ♣ A K 8 4

Bid just two spades even though you have a full opening bid! Your opponents are likely to have at least 18 points between them in high cards, so your prospects of game are negligible. Your partner did not double on the first round. He doubled on the second round, knowing that you have a good hand. He is only hoping for a part score, and if you now bid strongly in the hope of making a game, you are double-crossing him. (Pair your hand with the first one in this section and you'll see that two spades is the optimum spot; you'll have to work hard to make three, and four is impossible.)

3. *Free bids.* If your side has opened the bidding, any low-level bid is called a free bid if it immediately follows an opponent's bid. Suppose the bidding starts:

SOUTH	WEST	NORTH	EAST
1 ♦	1 ♡	?	

If North bids one spade, one notrump, two clubs, or two diamonds he is making a free bid because West's bid assured South of another chance to bid even if North now passes.

The old idea was that a free bid showed extra strength, but today this is only valid if the bid is specifically one notrump. A free response of one notrump should indicate 8-10 points instead of the usual 6-9, and it also promises a stopper in the opponent's suit.

In the great majority of cases, a free bid shows exactly the same strength as it would have following a pass. And there are three general situations in which a free bid is actually weaker than it would have been if the opponent had remained silent:

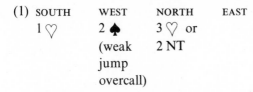

(1)

SOUTH	WEST	NORTH	EAST
1 ♡	2 ♠	3 ♡ or	
	(weak jump overcall)	2 NT	

If West had remained silent, North's bid would be a jump, forcing to game. But now that West has crowded the auction, North must relax the requirements for his bid or he may be shut out of the bidding entirely.

See how well this approach works with two possible North-South holdings:

(a)

NORTH
- ♠ 7 6
- ♡ K J 7 2
- ♢ Q 8 4 2
- ♣ K 7

SOUTH
- ♠ Q 4
- ♡ A Q 10 8 6
- ♢ K 7
- ♣ A J 10 4

(b)

NORTH
- ♠ K J 6
- ♡ 7 2
- ♢ A J 4 2
- ♣ Q 8 7 3

SOUTH
- ♠ Q 4
- ♡ A Q 10 8 6
- ♢ K 7
- ♣ A J 10 4

North should bid three hearts with hand (a) and two notrump with hand (b). In both cases, South will raise to game. But if North meekly passes over West's nuisance bid, two easy games will be missed.

As we have seen, the free, non-jump raise to three hearts is mildly encouraging and suggests a hand with perhaps 8–11 points. Similarly, the two-notrump bid without a jump shows 10–11 points. Both bids can be passed.

(2)	SOUTH	WEST	NORTH	EAST
	1 ♡	Dbl.	?	

Almost any action by North—one spade, two clubs or diamonds, two or three hearts—is weaker than it would have been if West had passed. Again, all these bids are likely to be passed by opener unless he has extra values.

The reason is that North has denied a good hand, say 10 points or more, by his failure to redouble. Any action other than a redouble therefore suggests less than 10 points.

SOUTH	WEST	NORTH	EAST
1 ♡	Dbl.	?	

You are North after this bidding. What do you bid in each case?

(a) ♠ K J 10 6 2
    ♡ 7 3
    ◇ 8 6
    ♣ J 10 8 2

(c) ♠ 8 7 6
    ♡ K 8 5 4
    ◇ Q 6 3 2
    ♣ 7 5

(b) ♠ 8 6
    ♡ 7 3
    ◇ J 10 8
    ♣ A Q J 8 4 2

(d) ♠ 8 7 6
    ♡ K 8 5 4
    ◇ K J 8 7 2
    ♣ 7

ANSWERS:
(a) *One spade.* This is not forcing and implies a 5-card suit.

(b) *Two clubs,* suggesting, but not guaranteeing, a 6-card suit, since you have gone to the two level.

(c) *Two hearts.* This is a very weak action.

(d) *Three hearts.* With useful support for hearts, some side values, and ruffing possibilities, you should pre-empt to make life difficult for the opponents.

That brings us to the last situation where, after an intervening call, your bid shows a weaker hand than otherwise:

(3) | SOUTH | WEST | NORTH | EAST |
|---|---|---|---|
| 1 ♡ | 1 NT | ? | |

West's bid shows 16–18 points and a heart stopper in a balanced hand, so your chances for game are slight indeed. But if you hold 9 or more points as North, your side holds more than half the deck (partner presumably has 13 points; added to your 9, this gives North-South 22 points). Moreover, it leaves just a point or two for East (your side has at least 22 points and West has shown at least 16), so West will have his hands full trying to play one notrump with a virtually worthless dummy. So with 9 points, North should double with pleasure and expect a handsome reward. It follows that if North instead bids his suit or raises South's, he has less than 9 points and no hope for game. South should therefore pass unless he has great distributional strength in reserve.

4. *Low-level penalty doubles.* It is not necessary to bid games and slams to earn large profits at the

bridge table. It is often possible to double the opponents at a low level and collect a penalty of 300 points, 500 points, or even more. For any penalty double of a notrump contract, you need to be reasonably certain that your side has more than half the high-card strength in the deck. To double a suit contract you should be reasonably sure that the hand is a misfit. Length and strength in the opponent's suit is only one factor. It is also desirable to be short in your partner's suit to insure that his honors there are not prematurely ruffed away.

Suppose the bidding begins:

SOUTH	WEST	NORTH	EAST
1 ♡	2 ◇	?	

Sitting North, you hold:

(a)	♠ Q 10 6	(b)	♠ 5
	♡ 5		♡ Q 10 6
	◇ K 10 8 3		◇ K 10 8 3
	♣ A J 7 6 2		♣ A J 7 6 2

Hand (a) is entirely suitable for a double of two diamonds. You know that your side has more than half the high-card strength, for your partner must have more than 10 points to open the bidding. And the hand seems to be a misfit because you are short in your partner's heart suit. (If your side has a misfit, chances are the opponents do also.) Lastly, you will be happy to double any new suit to which they try to escape.

Hand (b) would be a bad double of two diamonds. The strength is sufficient, but there is no evidence of a misfit. Your three cards in your partner's heart suit are a liability. Furthermore, the opponents might run from the double and find their spade fit. With this hand it is wiser to bid a simple two hearts over two diamonds.

5. *When you are doubled.* If your side has been doubled, the important thing is to avoid panic. Many small penalties turn into big ones because players jump from the frying pan to the fire—and perhaps back to the frying pan at a higher level.

   If your partner makes an overcall and is doubled, it is seldom right to rescue him into another suit. A rescue may be ventured at the same level only if you feel it probable that your suit is longer than your partner's suit. And if you must go to a higher level, you must be very sure of your ground.

   Let's see how well you have profited from this counsel:

WEST	NORTH	EAST	SOUTH
1 ♡	2 ♢	Dbl.	?

You are South with the following hands. What is your action?

(a) ♠ K 10 8 7 5 4 3   (b) ♠ 9 8 2
    ♡ 8 6   ♡ 8 6
    ♢ 5   ♢ 5
    ♣ 9 8 2   ♣ K 10 8 7 6 3 2

ANSWERS:

(a) *Two spades.* It is likely that you have more spades than your partner has diamonds.

(b) *Pass.* Three clubs would take you to a higher level, and is most likely to make matters worse.

When your side has been doubled for penalties at a low level, it never pays to redouble because you are sure your contract will succeed. You will be amply rewarded just making your doubled contract; a redouble may scare the opponents into a save that scores fewer points on your side of the ledger. Therefore, the redouble is used instead as an S.O.S.

SOUTH	WEST	NORTH	EAST
1 ◇	2 ♣	Dbl.	?

East's hand is:

♠ Q J 8 4 3   ♡ J 10 7 6 2   ◇ 10 8 3   ♣ –

With no trumps at all in the dummy, West will surely be in trouble in two clubs doubled. He is likely to have a 5- or 6-card club suit and so he will be outnumbered in trumps. East should reason that two spades or two hearts will be an improvement, but he cannot tell which.

Therefore, East should redouble, a conventional request to his partner to pick another suit. West will bid one of the major suits; even if he has to bid a doubleton suit the resulting contract should be an improvement on two clubs.

But a word of caution. Do not use this S.O.S. redouble with an unreliable partner who may pass because he is puzzled. Your redouble will then have turned misfortune into disaster, perhaps of 1000 points or more.

6. *The positional factor.* Your partner's bidding reveals the extent to which the hands fit, but it is not the sole factor that alters the potential of your hand. The opponents' bidding is also highly significant.

   Suppose you have the doubleton king of spades. If spades are bid on your right, a possible trick has become an almost certain trick. Your king is now worth an ace and can be valued accordingly.

   But if spades are bid on your left, your king is likely to be a dead duck. If you become the declarer, it may prevent a spade lead, and there is always the chance that your partner will produce the spade ace or queen, but nevertheless you must devalue your king. Deduct one or two points from the total strength of your hand. The same is true with many other holdings. An ace-queen is worth two tricks if the suit is bid to your right, but only one if it is bid to your left. And many combinations such as K–J–x and A–J–x vary similarly. Whenever an opponent bids a suit in which you have some honor strength, consider whether this should encourage or discourage you.

   If both opponents bid a suit in which you have three or four cards, you can judge that your partner is likely to have a singleton, perhaps even a void. If you have no high-card strength in the suit, aggressive bidding is called for: the high cards you have will all pull their weight if your side plays the hand. But if you have honor strength in the opponent's suit your hand is suited for defense: your honors will inconvenience the opponents if they play the hand but have little value in your contract.

7. *Bid one more.* When both sides have fair high-card strength and a powerful fit in one or two suits, the bidding is likely to be competitive to a high level. In such circumstances there is one golden rule: *When in doubt, bid one more.*

The reason for this is purely mathematical. If you think the opponents may make their contract of five clubs, but you are not sure, the odds in bidding one more are all in your favor. You will gain if either side can make a contract at the five-level; and your loss, if any, is small.

But if you let the opponents play their contract, you are risking the enormous loss which develops when it turns out that both sides can make their contracts. Assume both sides can make a vulnerable game. If you let the opponents play the hand, you may end up minus 600 points instead of plus 600 (for a total loss of 1200). If you bid on and find that neither side could make game, you are unlikely to lose more than 400 points. And if you bid one more "for luck," you may force the opponents to do the same.

At the slam level aggressiveness is even more rewarding.

Consider the following hand from an international match. A glance at the diagram shows that neither side can make a slam. Playing in hearts, North-South have two immediate diamond losers. Playing in spades, East-West can lose a club and a club ruff.

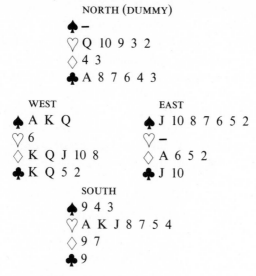

NORTH (DUMMY)
♠ —
♡ Q 10 9 3 2
◇ 4 3
♣ A 8 7 6 4 3

WEST
♠ A K Q
♡ 6
◇ K Q J 10 8
♣ K Q 5 2

EAST
♠ J 10 8 7 6 5 2
♡ —
◇ A 6 5 2
♣ J 10

SOUTH
♠ 9 4 3
♡ A K J 8 7 5 4
◇ 9 7
♣ 9

East-West vulnerable.

At one table the bidding was:

EAST	SOUTH	WEST	NORTH
3 ♠	4 ♡	4 NT	6 ♡
Pass	Pass	6 ♠	Dbl.
All pass			

North-South were happy with the result, because they beat six spades doubled by one trick
after South led his singleton club and ruffed the
return. But they had both bid badly. North should
not have doubled six spades, for he had no as-
surance that he could defeat that contract. And
South should have retreated into seven hearts,
lacking any vestige of defense outside the heart
suit.

When the hand was replayed, East passed and South bid four hearts. North eventually bid seven hearts, and was gloriously rewarded. West had no reason to know that a diamond lead was vital and he led a spade. Dummy ruffed and declarer attacked clubs. By ruffing clubs three times in his own hand he was able to establish winners in dummy on which his diamond losers eventually disappeared. Following the rule of bidding one more for luck gave North-South an enormous profit.

COMPETITIVE BIDDING QUIZ

1.

WEST	NORTH	EAST	SOUTH
1 ♡	Pass	Pass	?

What action do you take as South with each of the following hands:

(a) ♠ K 5 4 3 2 ♡ 10 8 4 ◇ Q J 5 ♣ A 4

(b) ♠ K 5 4 3 ♡ 8 4 ◇ A J 5 ♣ Q J 9 3

(c) ♠ K 5 4 ♡ Q 10 7 ◇ J 9 5 3 ♣ A Q 7

(d) ♠ 5 ♡ A Q 10 6 ◇ K J 8 4 ♣ A J 8 3

(e) ♠ A Q 8 7 6 3 ♡ 8 7 5 ◇ A K Q ♣ 7

(f) ♠ A K J 10 7 ♡ 9 ◇ A K Q 8 7 4 ♣ J

2.

NORTH	EAST	SOUTH	WEST
1 ♣	1 ♡	?	

What would you bid as South with each of the following hands:

(a) ♠ 8 5 3 2   ♡ 10 3 2   ◇ K Q 10 6   ♣ Q 5

(b) ♠ 9 8 4   ♡ 10 3 2   ◇ K Q 10 6 3   ♣ Q 5

(c) ♠ 10 3 2   ♡ K Q 10 6   ◇ 8 5 3 2   ♣ Q 5

(d) ♠ Q 5   ♡ 10 3 2   ◇ 8 5 3 2   ♣ K Q 10 6

(e) ♠ 10 3 2   ♡ K 5   ◇ K Q 10 6 3   ♣ J 5 4

(f) ♠ Q 10 7 3   ♡ –   ◇ K 7 2   ♣ A K 8 6 3 2

3.
NORTH	EAST	SOUTH	WEST
1 ♡	Dbl.	?	

What would you bid as South with each of the following hands:

(a) ♠ 8 5 3 2   ♡ Q 5   ◇ K J 6 3   ♣ 10 3 2

(b) ♠ 8 5 3 2   ♡ 10 3 2   ◇ K J 6 3   ♣ 8 5

(c) ♠ 8 5 3 2   ♡ K J 6 3   ◇ K 10 4 2   ♣ 6

(d) ♠ 8 5 3 2   ♡ K J 6 3 2   ◇ K J 4 2   ♣ –

(e) ♠ A 10 4   ♡ 5 2   ◇ K 10 4 2   ♣ J 8 6 3

(f) ♠ A Q 4   ♡ 5 4   ◇ K 10 4 2   ♣ J 8 6 3

ANSWERS TO COMPETITIVE BIDDING QUIZ

1. (a) *One spade.* Partner is marked with some strength by East's pass, and there is every reason to think that you can make a part score in spades.

   (b) *Double.* Not enough strength for a normal takeout double, but all actions are weaker than normal in the balancing position. You have some support for all unbid suits.

(c) *One notrump.* In the pass-out position the bid promises 11–14 points, not the customary 16–18 points of a notrump opening or direct overcall.

(d) *Pass.* Even with 15 points in high cards, it should pay to defend. You will do well against one heart, and should have no wish to hear anyone bid spades.

(e) *Two spades.* Encouraging but not forcing. This shows a substantially better hand and suit than the simple bid of one spade in example (a). *Double* should be the second choice.

(f) *Two hearts.* This is a game-forcing cue bid. You expect to play in four spades or five diamonds, or even in slam. The immediate cue bid enables you to make minimum bids on subsequent rounds to find your optimum contract. You should plan on showing your longer diamond suit first and then bidding spades twice, if convenient, to show it is a 5-carder.

2. (a) *One spade.* You have enough strength to make a bid of some kind, and one spade is the only possible action. A suit response at the one-level, whether or not the opponents have overcalled, simply shows 6 points or more and at least four cards in the suit. The strength of the suit is unimportant.

(b) *Pass.* You would like to bid, but there is just no convenient action. Two diamonds would promise 10 points or more, and you cannot support clubs or bid at the one-level.

(c) *One notrump.* This normally shows 8–10 points

and a heart stopper, but in this case the two tens and the position and solidity of the heart stopper is full compensation for the missing point.

(d) *Two clubs.* The overcall does not change the meaning of this single raise. It shows 6–9 points and, since it is a minor suit, at least four clubs.

(e) *Two diamonds.* One point short of the usual 10 for a new-suit bid at the two-level, but ample compensation: a strong 5-card suit, two tens, and a heart king which has been improved in value by the opposing bid.

(f) *Two hearts.* The cue bid at this early stage suggests a club fit and a slam, with control of the heart suit. (In other low-level situations, the cue bid merely shows game intentions and does not promise control.)

3. (a) *Pass.* Following a double, a suit bid promises a 5-card suit and a hand of some 4–9 points.

(b) *Two hearts.* Strain to raise partner's suit over a double. Here you raise even though lacking the values for a normal response.

(c) *Three hearts.* This is a pre-emptive action after a takeout double.

(d) *Four hearts.* We expect to make this, and we do not want the opponents in the bidding.

(e) *One notrump.* Just the hand for the bid, which shows a balanced hand with 8 or 9 points.

(f) *Redouble.* The normal action over a double with 10 points or more. It suggests the possibility of a penalty, so the opener should seldom take any action other than to double a rescue bid of the opponents.

The following deal is a test of competitive judgment:

NORTH (DUMMY)
♠ A 10 8 6
♡ 10 8 6
◇ J 9 6 5
♣ A K

WEST
♠ K J 7 4
♡ –
◇ A K 8
♣ Q J 10 9 7 4

EAST
♠ 3
♡ J 9 7 4 3 2
◇ Q 10 3 2
♣ 6 3

SOUTH
♠ Q 9 5 2
♡ A K Q 5
◇ 7 4
♣ 8 5 2

Neither side vulnerable

WEST	NORTH	EAST	SOUTH
1 ♣	Dbl.	1 ♡	Dbl.
1 ♠	Dbl.	2 ◇	Pass
Pass	Dbl.	Pass	2 NT
Dbl.	Pass	Pass	Redbl.
All pass	Pass	Pass	

Study the bidding, and consider the eleven positive actions. Which of the eleven do you agree with? And where you disagree, what alternative do you prefer?

The result of the deal was a disaster for East-West, for the final contract of two notrump redoubled could not be defeated.

West led the king of diamonds and continued diamonds. After the defense had made four diamond tricks, East shifted to the heart four.

South played low from his hand, confident that East held the heart jack, and won the trick in dummy. A low spade was led to the queen, and West's king was the last trick for the defense. The bidding had marked West with at least four spades, so South was sure of three spade tricks by running the nine at a later stage.

Now let's return to the eleven positive calls. The first six are logical:

1. West's one-club bid is normal.
2. North's takeout double is an acceptable minimum at this vulnerability, but a pass is also acceptable.
3. One heart by East is right, suggesting at least five hearts and fewer than 10 high-card points.
4. South's double is right, showing some strength and at least four hearts.
5. One spade by West is also right: he must escape from one heart doubled. An acceptable alternative with an expert partner is a redouble, which must be an S.O.S. demanding a takeout when partner has been doubled for penalties.
6. Double of one spade by North is right: any other action would deny holding four spades.

Now the auction departs from the straight and narrow course:

7. Two diamonds by East is wrong, but only slightly. Two clubs may be the best final contract for East-

West, since West probably has five or six clubs and is therefore unlikely to have four diamonds. One notrump may be best, as it leaves various doors open, but an S.O.S. redouble is allowable.

8. North's third double is right. He has four diamonds and the opponents are on the run.

9. South's two-notrump bid is wrong. He should either pass or bid two spades: his partner's earlier double showed four cards in spades, so that suit should be better than notrump even if West has bid the suit.

10. West's final double is wrong. His partner's bidding has not shown strength, so two notrump will be at best a close thing. One should not risk doubling the opponents into game for the sake of a possible 50 points. So do not make such doubles unless you are sure of at least a two-trick defeat.

11. South's final redouble is a borderline speculation based on the known strength of the North-South hands. Count it right, but also count a pass as correct.

If you got nine or ten right answers, your bidding judgment is excellent. Less than five right answers suggests some inexperience in this important area.

PART II

Mistakes in Play

Mistakes in Play

THERE IS nothing as discouraging to a bridge enthusiast than to bid a hand to perfection only to mess it up in the play. Most players have a convenient blind spot about their declarer play: if the hand fails, they chalk it up to bad luck, rationalizing that the line of play chosen was somehow superior to the one that would have succeeded.

The imagination of a declarer intent on losing a cold contract would seem to defy cataloguing. However, to bring order out of this chaos, we can pinpoint several areas where declarers err most frequently:

MISMANAGING SUIT COMBINATIONS

Even experienced players handle many common suit combinations in a routine fashion without taking the time to work out how many tricks they need and what opposing lies of the cards will spell success.

The average player has an even tougher time, since he is less familiar with these combinations and it takes him longer to figure out the right play. Fortunately, the effort is rewarding, for once a specific situation is mastered, it becomes part of the player's repertoire and is easily handled the next time it is encountered.

A careful study of the next several pages will help put the diligent reader on the right road to practical, winning play. Decide how you would handle the following examples before reading the explanations:

NORTH (DUMMY)

♣ K J 3 2

SOUTH

♣ Q 5 4

Most players rely on a 3–3 division of the opposing cards to produce three tricks here. However, entries permitting, declarer can give himself an extra chance by leading low cards twice from his hand toward dummy's honors. If West started with a doubleton ace, he will be forced to play it "on air." The king, queen, and jack will all make tricks, despite the 4–2 split of the suit.

Whenever there is a 4–3 holding with honors split between the two hands, declarer should try to lead twice toward the hand with the two honors.

NORTH (DUMMY)

♣ Q J 3 2

SOUTH

♣ A 5 4

Many players automatically lead the queen—or jack —for a finesse; this is the correct play if two quick tricks are all that are needed. But there is a far superior play if you are looking for three tricks in this suit and can afford to give up the lead: lead low cards twice from the South hand toward the queen-jack. This brings in three tricks whenever West holds the king, regardless of the distribution. (Practically any play works if the suit is divided 3–3.)

Theoretically, it is right to play the ace first, just in case East holds a singleton king, but in practice, it is more convenient to lead low immediately, saving the ace as the entry back for the second lead.

(a)   NORTH (DUMMY)
♣   A 4 3 2

SOUTH
♣   Q 5

(b)   NORTH (DUMMY)
♣   A K 3 2

SOUTH
♣   J 4

Most players know that they should lead low from dummy with these holdings, to have a chance to score the honor in the South hand. But what about this one:

NORTH (DUMMY)
♣ A Q 3 2

SOUTH
♣ J 4

Leading the jack for a finesse is good enough if only two tricks are needed, but the best chance for *three* tricks is to lead low toward the jack. This succeeds when East has K-x or K-x-x, for you can prevent his king from destroying your honor. If East plays low on the first trick, allowing the jack to win, duck the next round. Then play the ace on the third round. By this time, East will be out of clubs so your queen will stand up. In this fashion, you will win a trick with each of your three honors.

NORTH (DUMMY)
♣ A K 4 3 2

SOUTH
♣ Q 10

When one hand is long in a suit and the other has a doubleton including an honor, it is right to lead toward the doubleton. Here the immediate finesse of the ten is much better than playing the queen and hoping for a 3–3 break. (But declarer will need two side-suit entries to North—one for the finesse, the other to get back to play out the ace-king and the established small cards.)

The finesse succeeds 50 percent of the time and produces five tricks unless the suit breaks 5–1 or 6–0. Playing for a 3–3 division succeeds 36 percent of the time, about once in three.

Playing to the odds. You do not need to be a mathematician to play good bridge, but it helps to know your prospects in a few simple situations.

First, in finessing:

> One finesse
>> has one chance in two, or a 50% chance
>
> Two finesses
>> have one chance in four, or a 25% chance
>
> One finesse out of two
>> has three chances in four, or a 75% chance
>
> Two finesses out of three
>> have one chance in two, or a 50% chance

Second, in breaking a suit: An odd number of opposing cards tend to break favorably; that is, there is one card's difference between the opponents' holdings. An even number of cards tends to break unevenly; that is, one opponent has at least two more cards in the suit than the other. This is all you need remember and is illustrated by the following common suit divisions:

Missing	*They Will Divide*	*This Often*
Four cards	2–2	40%
	3–1	50%
	4–0	10%
Five cards	3–2	68%
	4–1	28%
	5–0	4%
Six cards	3–3	36%
	4–2	48%
	6–0	1%

Now let's return to more common suit distributions:

NORTH (DUMMY)
♣ A Q 10 2

SOUTH
♣ J 4 3

Be cautious about leading an honor for a finesse when a low card will do just as well. Entries permitting, declarer should lead low to finesse twice, preserving his jack. The lead of the jack would hold declarer to three tricks if West holds a singleton or doubleton king.

Switching the nine into the South hand illustrates another common error in play:

NORTH (DUMMY)

♣ A Q 10 2

SOUTH

♣ J 9 3

The lead of the jack is still incorrect, but for a different reason. Declarer need not conserve the jack as he has an abundance of high cards in clubs and would be only too happy to see West cover with the king. But it is wasteful of entries to lead the jack, for if West does not cover, the second lead of the suit must be won in dummy and South then needs an entry back to his hand to continue the finesse.

Nor does it help South to play the ten underneath the jack, for West may subsequently cover the nine; then, unless the suit breaks 3–3, the eight will become the master card on the fourth round.

All this is avoided by leading the nine, followed by the jack, on which the ten is played if West does not cover. This is the only sure way to win four tricks in the suit when West holds the king and South has the lead but no second entry to his hand.

In the following apparently easy situation, declarer can guard against a bad break:

NORTH (DUMMY)

♣ A K 10 3 2

SOUTH

♣ Q 9 5 4

Playing the ace or king reveals if either opponent started with J–x–x–x, and enables you to finesse through him when the other opponent shows out.

That may be obvious enough, but try this one:

NORTH (DUMMY)

♣ A K 9 3 2

SOUTH

♣ Q 8 5 4

The only danger is that one opponent may have all four missing cards. If they are with East, there is nothing to be done, but if West has them, the jack-ten can be trapped under the ace-king. So lead the queen first to uncover the situation. If East shows out, follow with a low card. West will no doubt play an honor, which you can top; you then return to the South hand in another suit to finesse again.

Very often, the right play in a suit will depend on whether you want the maximum number of tricks or are content with half a loaf:

NORTH (DUMMY)

♣ A J 3 2

SOUTH

♣ K 4 3

If you need four tricks, cash the king and finesse the jack, hoping for a 3–3 break and the queen with West. But if three tricks will suffice, it is right to play the ace and then the king before leading to the jack. You still make three tricks when West had the queen, or when the suit breaks 3–3. But your advantage is that you will pick up a doubleton queen whenever East has that holding.

NORTH (DUMMY)

♣ A 10 2

SOUTH

♣ Q 4 3

It is good to keep a second string in reserve. The only good play here is low from dummy to the queen. If this loses to the king, you can still finesse the ten later. This line produces two tricks unless the king is on the left and the jack on the right.

Many players go wrong by finessing the ten at the first trick. If this loses to the jack, there is no second chance for a finesse against the king.

NORTH (DUMMY)

♣ A K Q 10 2

SOUTH

♣ 3

The problem here is whether or not to take an immediate finesse. If five tricks are needed, the best chance is to finesse the ten. This succeeds whenever West hold J–x–x–x, but fails when East started with J–x–x. The first combination is more likely than the second, because the greater number of cards held in a given suit, the greater the probability that a specific card in that suit will be part of that holding.

Now, take the same diagram but let us say that North has no side entry. It may be prudent to play out the ace-king-queen to make sure of three tricks, while retaining some chance of five, rather than risk a losing first-round finesse that will prevent you from reaching dummy to take any club tricks.

There are many situations in which declarer must do some intelligent guessing. This is the most common:

NORTH (DUMMY)

♣ K 4 3 2

SOUTH

♣ Q 7 6 5

The only hope of making three tricks lies in finding one defender with a doubleton ace. So decide which one is more likely to have length or strength in the suit; perhaps the bidding or the play or the count of the other suits will provide a clue.

If East seems to be marked with most of the missing high-card strength, or to be shorter in the club suit, lead low from North, putting up the queen when East follows low. If this wins, duck the next round, hoping that East started with A–x and will now be forced to play his ace. Then, the king will pick up West's remaining club and you will have lost but one club trick.

However, you would lead low from the South hand to dummy's king if you felt West was more likely to hold the ace or to be short in clubs.

Do not be upset if your stellar play fails to bring in three tricks, for it is distinctly against the odds: not only must you find the ace with but one small card, but you must guess correctly which opponent holds it. Still, it is your only play for three tricks. If you do pull it off, you can modestly explain to the opponents that you have just executed a *finesse obligata,* so named because you are *obliged* to play low on the second trick.

NORTH (DUMMY)

♣ J 4 3 2

SOUTH

♣ Q 7 6 5

This is a guessing situation of the same type. You must guess which opponent has a doubleton honor, and arrange for him to play second to the trick when you lead the suit.

Suppose the player on the left has a doubleton ace or king. By leading from your hand you can make sure that his honor card is played "on air." He should play low the first time, and dummy's jack will lose, but you can duck next time to force his honor and establish two tricks in the suit.

This is a combination play that offers better prospects if the opponents will lead the suit. This is often true when it is possible that all four of the players have an honor card.

SUIT COMBINATION QUIZ

In each of the following problems, you can lead from either hand, have sufficient entries to get from one hand to the other at will, and do not mind surrendering the lead.

How do you play to give yourself the best chance for the maximum number of tricks?

1. NORTH (DUMMY)
   ♣ A Q 3 2
   SOUTH
   ♣ 6 5 4

2. NORTH (DUMMY)
   ♣ A K 3 2
   SOUTH
   ♣ J 5 4

3. NORTH (DUMMY)
   ♣ K 4 3 2
   SOUTH
   ♣ Q J 5

4. NORTH (DUMMY)
   ♣ K Q 3 2
   SOUTH
   ♣ 10 4

5. NORTH (DUMMY)
   ♣ A K 9 2
   SOUTH
   ♣ J 3

6. NORTH (DUMMY)
   ♣ A J 3 2
   SOUTH
   ♣ K 9

7. NORTH (DUMMY)
   ♣ A K J 10 9
   SOUTH
   ♣ 3 2

8. NORTH (DUMMY)
   ♣ Q 4 3 2
   SOUTH
   ♣ A 10

9. NORTH (DUMMY)
   ♣ A 10 2
   SOUTH
   ♣ Q 5 4 3

10. NORTH (DUMMY)
    ♣ A K 9 2
    SOUTH
    ♣ J 5 4 3

ANSWERS TO SUIT COMBINATION QUIZ

1. Not as easy as it looks, and few players get the right answer. *Lead low from dummy,* hoping that East will be helpful and play the king. If nothing like that happens, finesse the queen next time.

2. *Play the ace or king and then play low toward the jack.* If East is a poor player and plays low without thought, you can safely assume that he does not hold the queen; then it is right to duck the

second round, just in case West started with Q-x.

3. *Lead twice from dummy toward the queen-jack* to guard against A-x in East's hand. If the suit divides 3-3, any normal play produces three tricks.

4. *Lead low toward the ten;* this nets two tricks whenever East has the jack. If the ten loses to the jack, lead low to the queen. Assuming that wins, play low from North in case West's ace is now singleton.

5. *Lead low to the jack.* If it loses to the queen, finesse the nine the next time.

6. *Lead low from North to the nine.* This brings in three tricks if the ten is on the right; even when it is offside, there is a chance that the queen will fall under the ace on the third round.

7. *Finesse the jack, ten, or nine immediately,* planning a second finesse if the first one wins. Cashing the ace first fails when West has Q-x-x-x.

8. *Lead to the ten.* If it loses to the jack, play ace and then low, hoping that the king will fall on the third round.

9. *Lead from North to the queen.* If this loses to the king, finesse the ten later. This nets three tricks if the suit divides 3-3 and either missing honor is well-placed.

10. *For four tricks, play the ace and king,* hoping the queen will fall doubleton. But for three sure tricks, cash the ace and enter the South hand to lead to the nine. This insures three tricks against any distribution of the cards.

The following two deals illustrate advanced applications of the principles of suit combinations:

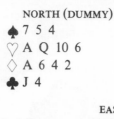

NORTH (DUMMY)
♠ 7 5 4
♡ A Q 10 6
♢ A 6 4 2
♣ J 4

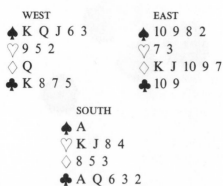

WEST
♠ K Q J 6 3
♡ 9 5 2
♢ Q
♣ K 8 7 5

EAST
♠ 10 9 8 2
♡ 7 3
♢ K J 10 9 7
♣ 10 9

SOUTH
♠ A
♡ K J 8 4
♢ 8 5 3
♣ A Q 6 3 2

North-South vulnerable.

SOUTH	WEST	NORTH	EAST
1 ♣	1 ♠	2 ♢	2 ♠
3 ♡	3 ♠	4 ♡	4 ♠
5 ♡	All pass		

The spade king was led, taken by the ace. Declarer then made the fine play of a low club from his hand. There was now no way to defeat the contract.

If West ducked, the jack would win, the two minor-suit aces would be cashed, and declarer would have cross-ruffed effectively—ruffing clubs with three high trumps in dummy and ruffing two spades low in his hand, to score, in all, two clubs, two outside aces, and seven trump tricks.

When the hand was actually played, West did his best by putting up the club king at the second trick and shifting to a trump, but declarer had the situation well in hand. He drew trumps, cashed the club jack, and now had three established club tricks, on which he discarded dummy's small diamonds. He thus scored four club tricks, four trumps tricks, one diamond ruff in dummy, and two side aces.

The defense fares no better if West plays a second spade after winning the club king. Declarer simply cashes the club jack before drawing trumps, ending in his hand, and the play continues as above.

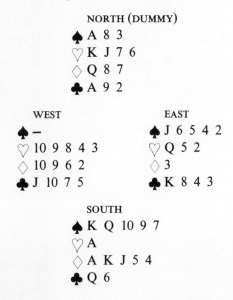

NORTH (DUMMY)
♠ A 8 3
♡ K J 7 6
♢ Q 8 7
♣ A 9 2

WEST
♠ —
♡ 10 9 8 4 3
♢ 10 9 6 2
♣ J 10 7 5

EAST
♠ J 6 5 4 2
♡ Q 5 2
♢ 3
♣ K 8 4 3

SOUTH
♠ K Q 10 9 7
♡ A
♢ A K J 5 4
♣ Q 6

In this historic deal from a Vanderbilt Cup final, Lee Hazen of New York bid to the sound contract of seven spades, just as his opponents did at the other table. But Hazen brought home the slam, while his opposite number did not.

In both cases, a heart was led, won by the ace. The only problem was to gather in the spade jack. The routine play, made at the other table, is to cash the king and then lead to the ace. This reveals the need for a finesse on the third round if West had a singleton and East, J–x–x–x. But it costs the contract in the actual case when East held all five outstanding spades, for it left but one trump in dummy when two trump finesses were necessary.

Hazen saw that it would cost him nothing to lead immediately to the spade ace, since he had spare entries to dummy. His play revealed West's void while retaining two small trumps to finesse twice against East's remaining J–x–x–x. East's trumps were picked up without further difficulty and the grand slam was scored.

MISMANAGING TRUMP

The basic decision which faces every declarer when dummy appears is whether to draw trumps. A simple rule works nine times out of ten:

Draw trumps unless dummy has a side suit which offers a ruffing possibility.

In other words, declarer should first look at dummy's short suit or suits. If he has greater length in that suit in his own hand, there is a potential ruff.

Suppose that spades are trump in this situation:

NORTH (DUMMY)
♠ 7 5 2
♣ 3 2

SOUTH
♠ A K 8 4 3
♣ 6 5 4

Unless another suit in dummy offers prospects of discarding clubs, your plan should be to lead clubs as quickly as possible. The defenders will no doubt shift to trumps to try to prevent the ruff, but declarer will be one jump ahead. He can lead a third round of clubs, ruffing in dummy, before the defenders can lead three rounds of trump.

When declarer holds the ace of the suit he plans to ruff, he usually ought to surrender the first trick.

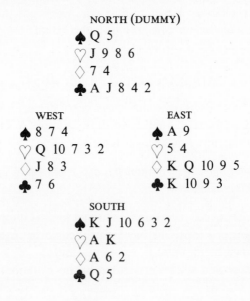

NORTH (DUMMY)
♠ Q 5
♡ J 9 8 6
◇ 7 4
♣ A J 8 4 2

WEST
♠ 8 7 4
♡ Q 10 7 3 2
◇ J 8 3
♣ 7 6

EAST
♠ A 9
♡ 5 4
◇ K Q 10 9 5
♣ K 10 9 3

SOUTH
♠ K J 10 6 3 2
♡ A K
◇ A 6 2
♣ Q 5

Neither side vulnerable.

EAST	SOUTH	WEST	NORTH
1 ◇	Dbl.	Pass	2 ♣
Pass	2 ♠	Pass	3 ♡
Pass	3 ♠	Pass	4 ♠
All pass			

West leads a diamond to East's queen and South ducks. To avert a diamond ruff, East must lead the spade ace followed by a second round. South can now draw the last trump and try the club finesse. The queen is led and East can take his king for his side's third trick, but declarer can discard his losing diamond on dummy's club jack—and wins the rest of the tricks.

(If East cannily plays low on the first club lead, declarer should not greedily repeat the club finesse. Since he has avoided a club loser, he can afford a second diamond loser. But it would be fatal to lose the *second* club finesse, for he would never get to dummy to cash the club ace.)

Declarer made his contract by keeping control of the diamond suit while retaining his chance for a diamond ruff. Even though the defense promptly shifted to trumps, he had an alternate line of play that saw him through. But if he had won the first diamond lead and played another diamond, East would play ace and another round of trump, and, when he wins the club king, he is able to defeat the contract by cashing another diamond.

It might seem that declarer can get home by winning the first diamond and trying the club finesse right away. But West plays the club seven—signaling that he has a doubleton (see page 199 for *length signals*)—so East wins his king and returns a club. This severs declarer's communications with dummy. If he doesn't play his club honor now, he will never win it; and if he does play it, West will ruff it.

Declarer's best shot now is to go back to diamonds, but East wins and plays ace and another trump. Declarer wins in dummy, but since West still has one trump remaining, declarer is still unable to score the club jack.

In short, the defense has an answer to any play of declarer—except if he ducks the opening diamond lead.

Sometimes a ruffing possibility is concealed. How would you play the following hand at six spades after the lead of the diamond queen?

NORTH (DUMMY)
♠ Q 5
♡ J 8 7 6 3 2
♢ A 8 2
♣ Q 7

SOUTH
♠ A K J 10 8 2
♡ 4
♢ K 6 4
♣ A K 5

Did you win the diamond king at trick one and try to establish the heart suit? If so, you are down one! The defense played a second diamond on winning your lead of a low heart. That knocked out your diamond entry to dummy. You still have two black queens as tries to dummy—and they are just enough to set up the heart suit by ruffing, for hearts break 4–2. But you cannot get back to dummy to use the good hearts.

The worst part is that you have gone down on an easy hand by overlooking a concealed ruffing possibility. The one side suit where dummy has fewer cards than declarer—clubs—has no losers, and there is surely no purpose in ruffing out a club *winner*. But what about discarding a diamond from dummy on declarer's third club? Then you can play ace-king of diamonds and ruff a diamond with dummy's trump queen. As long as you do not run into a bizarre break in one of the minor suits, you are assured of the slam, simply by transferring the ruff from clubs to diamonds.

Here's another case where the vital ruff is in dummy's card suit:

NORTH (DUMMY)
♠ K J 4
♡ 8 7 2
♢ K Q 2
♣ J 7 6 2

SOUTH
♠ A Q 10 9 5
♡ A 9 6 5
♢ J 8 3
♣ A

You reach four spades and the club king is led. This a good contract, but most players have a blind spot about this type of hand. Dummy has no ruff in sight, the usual play is to draw trumps and hope that the

hearts break 3–3. This offers only about one chance i
three of success.

Yet the contract is a virtual certainty by ruffing you
fourth round of hearts. At the second trick, play th
ace of hearts. Continue with hearts at every opportunit
Eventually, you can ruff the fourth round of hearts wit
a high trump. Of course, if the defense has opened
trump, and they played trumps when you let them i
with hearts, dummy's trumps would be exhausted be
fore you could ruff a heart. The defense would then t
one tempo ahead.

Exceptions to the rule. There are two situatio
where you may properly choose to draw trumps im
mediately, even though dummy has ruffing possibilitie

(1) With a combined holding of nine or more trump
between your two hands: There is now little dang
that dummy will run out of trumps needed f
ruffing. Therefore, it is usually safe to draw trum
early and arrange your ruffs later.

(2) When declarer plans to discard his losers on
long, solid, or establishable suit in dummy: H
may want to pull the outstanding trumps first
protect his side-suit winners. Even in this case, h
may choose to delay trump plays until he ha
tested how dummy's suit breaks. If he encounte
a bad break, he may still be able to fall back o
the ruffing alternative.

Exceptions in the other direction are more frequen
Even when there is no ruffing potential, declarer shoul
postpone drawing trumps in the following cases:

(1) It may be urgent to take a quick discard:
trumps are played first, the defense may gain th

lead and grab a vital trick before declarer can discard his loser.

(2) If dummy has the lead but is short of entries, it may be more important to use this chance to lead toward declarer's hand before drawing trumps.

(3) When dummy's entry to his establishable side suit is a trump, it may be necessary to establish the side suit first so as to retain the vital trump entry.

(4) If declarer has a feeble trump suit—seven cards, or, unhappily, less in the combined hands—he should normally leave the trump suit alone and wait for tricks to come to him. An attempt to draw trumps may leave the defenders in control.

Here are some challenging examples of trump management:

NORTH (DUMMY)
♠ 8 7 4 3
♡ 8 6 5 2
♢ K 3
♣ A 10 5

WEST
♠ Q J 10 2
♡ Q J 10
♢ A 8 2
♣ 6 4 3

EAST
♠ 6
♡ K 9 7 4 3
♢ 9 6 4
♣ J 9 8 2

SOUTH
♠ A K 9 5
♡ A
♢ Q J 10 7 5
♣ K Q 7

SOUTH	WEST	NORTH	EAST
1 ◇	Pass	1 ♡	Pass
2 ♠	Pass	3 ♠	Pass
4 ♠	All pass		

West leads the heart queen, and South wins with the ace. The contract seems easy, and you would expect to make an overtrick, losing only one spade and one diamond. Yet, the side suit must be established before drawing trumps or the contract will go down because of the bad trump break.

Accordingly, declarer leads to the diamond king at the second trick, which wins. He plays to his spade ace—for he can afford one round of trump without losing control. He continues with diamonds until West takes his ace. West plays another heart, forcing declarer to ruff. Now it is safe to cash the spade king, revealing the 4-1 break. But declarer goes back to diamonds, playing out his established suit. West can ruff the fourth round and draw South's last trump, but, in the meantime, dummy's hearts have all disappeared and dummy retains a trump to ruff a heart lead. So declarer easily takes the rest of the tricks.

See what happens if declarer had made the mistake of cashing two high trumps immediately: When West wins his diamond ace, he could draw all of the North-South trump with his queen-jack. Then there is nothing to stop the run of East's hearts—assuming he hasn't discarded any on the trump leads. The outcome would be a four-trick set!

When declarer and dummy each have four trumps, it may be easier to find the right play by looking at the combined holdings in reverse. From the North side, it is apparent that South's diamonds must be established while keeping control of the trump suit. Therefore, trump must not be drawn prematurely in case they break unfavorably.

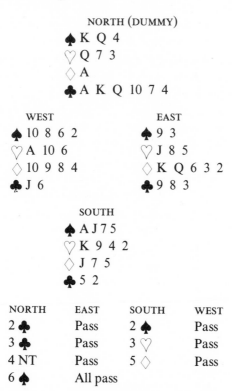

NORTH (DUMMY)
♠ K Q 4
♡ Q 7 3
♢ A
♣ A K Q 10 7 4

WEST
♠ 10 8 6 2
♡ A 10 6
♢ 10 9 8 4
♣ J 6

EAST
♠ 9 3
♡ J 8 5
♢ K Q 6 3 2
♣ 9 8 3

SOUTH
♠ A J 7 5
♡ K 9 4 2
♢ J 7 5
♣ 5 2

NORTH	EAST	SOUTH	WEST
2 ♣	Pass	2 ♠	Pass
3 ♣	Pass	3 ♡	Pass
4 NT	Pass	5 ♢	Pass
6 ♠	All pass		

West leads the diamond ten, and South has an interesting problem in control. If he draws trumps and they divide 4–2, the slam will be set. He can run off eleven tricks, but when he finally leads a heart, the defenders will take the last two tricks in the red suits. Foreseeing this, declarer should establish a heart trick before drawing trump—while dummy has a trump to deal with a second diamond lead. But the obvious play of leading to the heart king will fail. West will win the heart king with the ace and play a second diamond. Dummy must ruff, and South has no way to draw trumps, which are blocked in dummy.

The winning play is unusual: South must lead the heart *queen* from dummy at the second trick. West wins—declarer would abandon the suit and draw trumps if he ducked—and plays a second diamond. Now declarer ruffs in dummy, cashes the king-queen of trumps, and has the heart king as an entry to his own hand to draw the rest of the trumps.

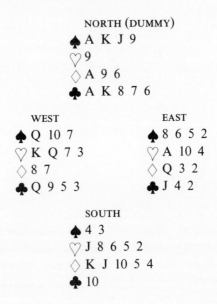

```
                    NORTH (DUMMY)
                    ♠ A K J 9
                    ♡ 9
                    ♢ A 9 6
                    ♣ A K 8 7 6

   WEST                            EAST
   ♠ Q 10 7                        ♠ 8 6 5 2
   ♡ K Q 7 3                       ♡ A 10 4
   ♢ 8 7                           ♢ Q 3 2
   ♣ Q 9 5 3                       ♣ J 4 2

                    SOUTH
                    ♠ 4 3
                    ♡ J 8 6 5 2
                    ♢ K J 10 5 4
                    ♣ 10
```

Ely Culbertson played this hand in six diamonds, back in 1935, against a club lead, won in dummy. Trumps could not be drawn because heart ruffs in dummy were needed. So, at trick two, the heart nine was led to prepare the way. East put up the ace, and, unwilling to jeopardize a potential trick by leading away from his trump queen, he led a second club.

South won in dummy, discarding a heart. He ruffed a club, then a heart, and cashed the two winning spades. A spade ruff and another heart ruff reduced all the players to four cards:

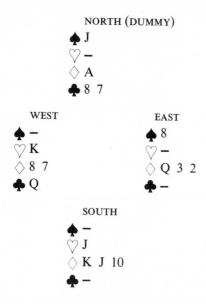

NORTH (DUMMY)
♠ J
♡ —
♢ A
♣ 8 7

WEST
♠ —
♡ K
♢ 8 7
♣ Q

EAST
♠ 8
♡ —
♢ Q 3 2
♣ —

SOUTH
♠ —
♡ J
♢ K J 10
♣ —

East may have thought he would make a trump trick, but he was soon disillusioned when declarer merrily continued his cross-ruff. A club was ruffed with the diamond ten, as East discarded his spade. The heart jack was ruffed with the diamond ace, as East helplessly under-ruffed. His queen-three of trumps was trapped by the lead from dummy at the twelfth trick.

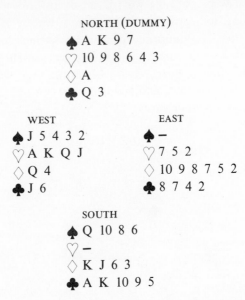

NORTH (DUMMY)
♠ A K 9 7
♡ 10 9 8 6 4 3
◇ A
♣ Q 3

WEST
♠ J 5 4 3 2
♡ A K Q J
◇ Q 4
♣ J 6

EAST
♠ —
♡ 7 5 2
◇ 10 9 8 7 5 2
♣ 8 7 4 2

SOUTH
♠ Q 10 8 6
♡ —
◇ K J 6 3
♣ A K 10 9 5

In a cross-ruff, declarer tries to make as many trumps as possible, but separately, and the defenders do best to lead trumps at every chance.

On this deal, South reached a six-spade contract, greedily doubled by West. His double would have gained points if he had followed through with a trump lead.

Instead he opened the heart king, and South ruffed. A diamond to the ace gave dummy entry for another heart ruff, and the club queen was the entry for still a third heart ruff. Dummy's remaining club was discarded on the diamond king to prepare for an over-ruffing situation if West had started with a singleton club.

South then led out his club winners and over-ruffed in dummy when West ruffed the third round of the suit. A final heart ruff—with the trump queen—assured the slam, for dummy's ace-nine of spades were sure winners. In all, declarer scored two club tricks, two diamond tricks, and *eight* trumps. Had West opened a trump, declarer would have been limited to seven trump tricks.

WASTING ENTRIES

In forming his plan of play, declarer will usually discover that he needs a certain number of entries to each hand. Generally, declarer's is the stronger hand and dummy's, the one short of entries that may be needed to establish and cash a side suit or to take finesses to declarer's hand.

Sometimes, the entries are apparent and declarer's task is just to preserve them until the proper time. Other times, the entries are hidden or must be manufactured. In these latter cases, the casual player often goes astray.

Suppose a club is opened into this suit:

NORTH (DUMMY)
♣ K J 2

SOUTH
♣ A Q 3

Your aim should be to leave a zigzag sequence of honors from one hand to the other and back, so that you can overtake an honor if needed.

If you need later entries to dummy—or if you want the lead immediately in your hand—win with the ace. This leaves two entries to dummy—or one to each hand, as you choose.

When you need entries to your own hand later—or if you want dummy in the lead right away—win with the jack. Now you have the later option of two entries to your hand—or one to each hand.

But winning the first trick with either the king or queen is a clear mistake, because it limits the overtaking possibilities and thus reduces the flexibility.

Hidden entries can also be developed with small spot cards:

NORTH (DUMMY)
♣ A 6 4 3

SOUTH
♣ K Q 8 2

The top cards clearly provide two entries to declarer's hand and one to dummy. But the fourth round of the suit may be important.

If declarer needs an extra entry to dummy eventually, he must get rid of the eight under dummy's ace. Let's assume the suit splits 3-2, as it will two-thirds of the time. Now the deuce can be led to dummy's six to enter dummy on the fourth round.

See if you can solve the entry problem on this hand:

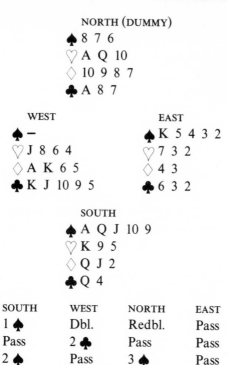

NORTH (DUMMY)
♠ 8 7 6
♡ A Q 10
◇ 10 9 8 7
♣ A 8 7

WEST
♠ –
♡ J 8 6 4
◇ A K 6 5
♣ K J 10 9 5

EAST
♠ K 5 4 3 2
♡ 7 3 2
◇ 4 3
♣ 6 3 2

SOUTH
♠ A Q J 10 9
♡ K 9 5
◇ Q J 2
♣ Q 4

SOUTH	WEST	NORTH	EAST
1 ♠	Dbl.	Redbl.	Pass
Pass	2 ♣	Pass	Pass
2 ♠	Pass	3 ♠	Pass
4 ♠	All pass		

North-South struggle into four spades. As declarer, you are not unhappy until West cashes the king-ace of diamonds and East ruffs the third round. But you reflect that if the trump king is onside, you can still bring home the skimpy game.

East leads back a club and your queen is covered by the king. You win with dummy's ace and finesse in trumps, but get a rude shock when West shows out.

East now has K-x-x of trump remaining, so you need three entries to dummy—two to pick up the trumps and one to cash the fourth diamond for a club discard. But dummy apparently has only two entries—the ace and queen of hearts. Can you manufacture the third and vital entry?

Yes; if West has the heart jack—likely in view of his takeout double—a heart finesse to the ten will produce the extra entry.

You cross your fingers and decide to test your luck right away. You lead the heart five at the sixth trick, play the ten from dummy and breathe a sigh of relief when it wins. Now you finesse in trumps, play the heart nine to the queen for the last trump finesse, and draw the last trump with the ace, while the ace of hearts is still in dummy as entry to the winning diamond.

Of course, this play would lead to defeat if East produced the heart jack, but the loss of an extra trick is a small price to pay.

If you want to postpone the fateful moment, you can take the heart finesse later, but you must be careful. A winning play is to overtake the king with the ace at the first trick and later finesse to the ten. But if you carelessly lead low to dummy's queen initially, West can thwart your plans on the next heart lead by going up with his jack to force the ace. Now South's king must win the third round and dummy's third heart entry has vanished. Would he make such a play? It is not so very unlikely after you go into deep study on winning the first trump finesse: He too has time to think, and may conclude that you are desperate for entries to dummy.

Here is a test of entry timing:

NORTH (DUMMY)
♠ 8 6 4 2
♡ 6 5 4 3
♢ A 3
♣ A 7 5

WEST	EAST
♠ Q 10 7 3	♠ J 9 5
♡ J 10 9 2	♡ K 8
♢ 6	♢ J 10 9 2
♣ J 8 6 3	♣ 10 9 4 2

SOUTH
♠ A K
♡ A Q 2
♢ K Q 8 7 5 4
♣ K Q

SOUTH	WEST	NORTH	EAST
2 ♢	Pass	3 ♢	Pass
3 NT	Pass	4 NT	Pass
6 NT	All pass		

You receive the lead of the heart jack. After this favorable start, you may think that thirteen tricks are in sight. But stop to think what will happen if diamonds do not break 3–2.

If you go after the overtrick, you will lose your small slam! After clearing the two high clubs from your hand, you cross to dummy's diamond ace to cash a third club. The second diamond lead discloses the dreaded 4–1 break. Now you must let East in with a diamond in order to establish your small diamonds. When you do, he cashes a club to put you down one.

The problem can be solved by surrendering a diamond trick at the right moment—while the diamond ace remains in dummy as later entry to the club ace. But an immediate duck of a diamond trick might fail, for the defense might return a diamond, using up dummy's entry while the clubs are blocked.

The solution is to cash the king-queen of clubs immediately and then to duck a diamond. This permits declarer to lose a diamond trick while he still has club control and an entry to dummy. This is the certain play, unless diamonds were 5–0, in which case nothing would help.

The overtrick is the premium you pay for insurance.

FAILURE TO PLAN AND
HASTY PLAY AT TRICK ONE

Many hands are needlessly set because declarer did not take time out to plan his play when dummy was put down. Often the crucial play must be made at the first trick; the second trick may be too late.

NORTH (DUMMY)
♠ A 4
♡ 8 7 5
♢ K 10 3
♣ A J 10 9 3

SOUTH
♠ K 8 7
♡ K J 4
♢ A 6 5 4
♣ Q 5 2

The three of hearts is led against a contract of three notrump. Since the heart deuce is missing, declarer cannot tell whether the lead was from a 5-card or a 4-card suit.

East plays the heart queen, and declarer should stop and think. He will then see that he needs just four club tricks for his contract, but there is no way to keep East off lead if he holds the guarded club king. He also sees that a heart lead from East could prove quite embarrassing.

An impulsive declarer hasn't time for such thoughts. He simply wins the heart king, takes the club finesse, and, when East leads a heart through declarer's jack-four, West cashes four heart tricks to set the contract. An unlucky hand?

Not at all. The thoughtful declarer holds up the heart king at the first trick, allowing the queen to win. East continues hearts and West ducks, saving his ace. Now declarer takes the club finesse without fear. If East has a third heart to lead, it means that West started with only four cards in the suit, so declarer loses but three hearts and one club.

The danger in the hand is that West started with five hearts. But, in that case, East started with two and has none remaining to lead back when he wins his club king.

Some readers, eager to find new rules, will conclude from this deal that it is best to hold up when declarer's weakest suit is opened in a notrump contract and the queen is played to his K–J–x. By switching the ace and queen of clubs, we can show how false such a rule would be:

NORTH
♠ A 4
♡ 8 7 5
♢ K 10 3
♣ Q J 10 9 3

SOUTH
♠ K 8 7
♡ K J 4
♢ A 6 5 4
♣ A 5 2

Again, the heart three is led to East's queen and again declarer needs but four club tricks. However, this time, he can keep East off lead while developing clubs. So it is correct to win the first trick with the heart king as this insures a second heart stopper should West lead the suit again.

The correct play is to enter dummy at trick two with the diamond king—or spade ace—and lead a club honor for a finesse, continuing with a second club finesse if the first one wins. If the finesse loses to West, he cannot attack hearts profitably.

Declarer is thus sure of his contract unless East has the club king guarded three times, in which case it cannot be picked up.

The right play in the club suit avails naught if not coupled with the right play in the heart suit. It all goes to prove that there is no substitute for thoughtful analysis before playing to the first trick. A second moral: The right play in one suit often depends upon the layout of a second key suit.

Declarer should be wary of hurrying to cash sure tricks. At a notrump contract, it is seldom right to take tricks immediately which are available at any time. Cashing an established suit will usually be a mistake, because it clarifies the situation for the defenders and deprives declarer of entries he may need later.

NORTH (DUMMY)
♠ 7 6 3
♡ Q 7
♢ J 5 2
♣ A K Q J 7

SOUTH
♠ A K J
♡ J 8 6 4 3
♢ Q 10
♣ 8 6 2

A spade is led against your contract of three notrump and you win with the jack. You are now sure of eight tricks, and it is tempting to cash five club tricks immediately. The right play here is to lead your shortest combined suit, diamonds. The diamond jack will be your ninth trick unless the defenders play hearts and give you a trick there instead. But if you run the clubs first, you would have no entry to dummy's diamonds, and the defense could take a spade trick and four winners in the red suits.

In a suit contract, on the other hand, it is usually best to discard losers quickly, but there are exceptions. If the declarer is not sure what he should discard, it may be wiser to postpone the decision:

NORTH (DUMMY)
♠ J 9 2
♡ A 7
♢ A 9 8 7
♣ K Q 7 4

WEST
♠ K 6 5 3
♡ Q J 6 3
♢ 5 4
♣ 9 6 3

EAST
♠ 10 4
♡ 10 9 8 5 4 2
♢ Q
♣ A 10 8 2

SOUTH
♠ A Q 8 7
♡ K
♢ K J 10 6 3 2
♣ J 5

SOUTH	WEST	NORTH	EAST
1 ♢	Pass	3 ♢	Pass
3 ♠	Pass	4 ♡	Pass
4 ♠	Pass	6 ♢	All pass

After North's forcing raise to three diamonds, South makes a natural bid of three spades. North's four hearts is a cue bid, showing control of hearts and a suitable hand for slam purposes. South focuses attention on a possible weakness in the unbid club suit by a cue bid of four spades, and North jumps to six diamonds because he has no fear of two immediate club losers. (Note that it would be a mistake for South to use Blackwood when he has two quick club losers.)

A black-suit lead would help South, but West leads a trump. South sees that he can discard a spade or a club on dummy's heart ace, but he cannot tell at this time which will be better. He therefore postpones the decision and leads to the diamond ace in dummy in order to make the key play of the club four.

We christened this maneuver the "Morton's Fork Coup," after the Cardinal who collected cash contributions on behalf of Henry VII of England. The ostentatious citizen was relieved of the wealth which he paraded, while his frugal neighbor was parted from the money he was presumably saving.

In this case, East can choose between spending his ace or saving his ace, but neither play offers salvation.

If he puts up the club ace and leads a spade, South wins with the ace, declining the finesse. He then cashes the heart king and club jack, enters dummy with a third round of trumps in order to discard his three remaining spades on dummy's king, queen of clubs, and ace of hearts.

If East saves the club ace—by playing low on the club lead—South adopts a different plan. He wins with the jack, cashes the heart king, and leads a trump to enter dummy. Now it is the club loser which is discarded on the heart ace. The spade king is the only trick for the defense.

What if West had the club ace? Then the winning play is to lead a low club from the *South* hand for the same glorious result. As long as you can guess which opponent holds the club ace, you can insure your slam by leading a low club through him before cashing the heart ace. South's discard on the heart ace is then determined by the arm of the fork on which the defender chooses to impale himself.

Cutting the opponents' communications is one of the most satisfying plays in the game, and is often missed through lack of foresight:

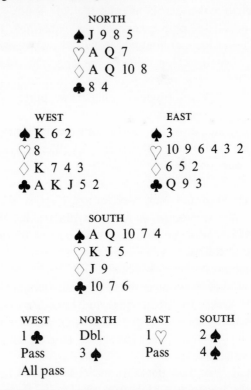

NORTH
♠ J 9 8 5
♡ A Q 7
♢ A Q 10 8
♣ 8 4

WEST
♠ K 6 2
♡ 8
♢ K 7 4 3
♣ A K J 5 2

EAST
♠ 3
♡ 10 9 6 4 3 2
♢ 6 5 2
♣ Q 9 3

SOUTH
♠ A Q 10 7 4
♡ K J 5
♢ J 9
♣ 10 7 6

WEST	NORTH	EAST	SOUTH
1 ♣	Dbl.	1 ♡	2 ♠
Pass	3 ♠	Pass	4 ♠
All pass			

West leads the club king and then shifts to the heart eight. This is likely to be a singleton, especially in light of the bidding: It is clear that East has bid with negligible high-card strength, so he is likely to have a 6-card heart suit as compensation.

South can confidently place the missing ace and two

kings on his left as part of West's opening bid. If West is a good player, he is likely to find the right defense after declarer routinely starts to draw trumps. On winning the spade king, he will no doubt underlead his ace of clubs to maneuver a heart ruff. West's only chance for a set is to find East with the club queen as the vital entry for the heart return.

South should anticipate this defense and plan a way to frustrate it. He wins the heart shift in his hand, and cashes his spade ace, since a spade finesse offers no hope. The jack of diamonds is then led for a finesse, and the suit continued for a second finesse when West rightly holds off.

South discards a club on the diamond ace, and makes the key play of continuing with the diamond queen. If East is able to ruff, South can over-ruff or discard as he pleases: the spade king is then the only trump left in the defenders' hands, so the risk of a heart ruff with a small trump has vanished.

But when East discards, South throws his remaining club, allowing the diamond king to win. This is a loser-on-loser play which cuts the defenders' communications. There is now no way for East to gain the lead, so West's heart ruff does not materialize and West's small trump can be extracted at South's leisure.

Notice the importance of cashing the spade ace before playing diamonds. Without that play, an astute East can ruff the fourth round of diamonds with his singleton trump—even though he knows his partner holds the master diamond—while West retains his small trump for a heart ruff, and the defense has the last laugh.

PLANNING QUIZ

Plan your play as declarer, sitting South, in each of the following deals:

1.   NORTH (DUMMY)
                      ♠ A J 7 3
                      ♡ Q J 9
                      ◇ Q
                      ♣ A K 8 7 3

                      SOUTH
                      ♠ 9 6 2
                      ♡ A 7 4
                      ◇ K J 10 9 6
                      ♣ J 4

Contract: 3 NT
Opening lead: ♡ 2

If the heart jack or queen is played at trick one, East will cover with the king.

2.   NORTH (DUMMY)
                      ♠ 7
                      ♡ K 10 6
                      ◇ A K 4 3
                      ♣ A J 8 6 2

                      SOUTH
                      ♠ K 8 4 3
                      ♡ A Q J 7 5
                      ◇ 8 7 2
                      ♣ 9

Contract: 4 ♡
Opening lead: ♡ 9

3.   NORTH (DUMMY)
                           ♠ 9 7 5
                           ♡ A J 4 3
                           ◇ K Q J
                           ♣ 6 3 2

                           SOUTH
                           ♠ A 10 2
                           ♡ K Q 9 8 5 2
                           ◇ 5 3
                           ♣ K 4

Contract: 3 ♡
Opening lead: ♠ Q

West overcalled with two clubs. East plays the spade eight on the first trick.

4.   NORTH (DUMMY)
                           ♠ A K 5
                           ♡ 8
                           ◇ K J 10 7 3
                           ♣ A Q 7 6

                           SOUTH
                           ♠ Q J 4 3
                           ♡ A 7 2
                           ◇ Q 9 4
                           ♣ 5 4 2

Contract: 4 ♠
Opening lead: ♡ 3

East overcalled with one heart.

5.

NORTH (DUMMY)

♠ A 6 5
♡ 8 7 6 3 2
♢ A J 9 6 4
♣ —

SOUTH

♠ K 8 4
♡ —
♢ K Q 10 8 2
♣ 9 8 7 5 3

Contract: 6 ♢, doubled
Opening lead: ♡ K

The auction has been competitive: West has shown a strong hand, including a heart suit.

6.

NORTH (DUMMY)

♠ K J 5 3
♡ K 7 6
♢ A 4 2
♣ K Q 3

SOUTH

♠ A 9 7 6
♡ A Q 8 2
♢ K Q
♣ A 10 5

Contract: 6 ♠
Opening lead: ♡ J

ANSWERS TO PLANNING QUIZ

1. *Play the jack or queen and let the king hold!*
   Whatever the defenders do, you can overtake the
   diamond queen with the king to establish that
   suit, and the heart ace will remain as an entry to
   your hand to run the established diamonds. Of
   course, if a heart is returned at the second trick,
   you win in dummy.

2. The trump lead was good for the defense, but it
   at least suggests that the trumps are breaking well.
   West would be unlikely to lead a trump from a
   singleton or a 4-card holding.

   The right plan is a dummy reversal. South
   should win with the heart ace, lead to the club
   ace, and ruff a club. Then he should cross twice
   to the dummy in diamonds to ruff two more clubs
   with the queen-jack of hearts. If the clubs break
   4–3, dummy has a club winner by this time, so
   South leads his last trump. Dummy's king-ten
   pull the trumps, assuming a normal break, and
   the fifth club in dummy is South's tenth trick.

3. *Let the spade queen win;* if West continues spades,
   let him—but not East—win the second trick. West
   no doubt has both minor-suit aces as part of the
   strength shown by his overcall, and the defense
   will take five tricks if East is given the opportunity to lead a club through your king-four.
   Eventually, you will discard a club on dummy's
   third diamond: Your objective is to keep East off
   lead until then.

4. *An unexpected ducking play. By allowing East
   to win the first heart, you keep control.* If he plays

a second heart, you ruff in dummy and play ace-king of trumps. You return to your hand in diamonds by leading low to the nine. (If that loses to the ace, the diamond queen provides the needed entry.) Now you finish drawing trumps, and can establish and cash the diamonds while the heart ace is still available as a stopper.

If you win the first trick, you may still make the contract if the trumps kindly break 3-3, but you will give yourself plenty of problems if they break 4-2.

5. South must not allow pleasure in his contract to blind him to reality. *His first move, after ruffing the first trick, should be to cash the ace and king of spades.* He can then cross-ruff happily, conceding a spade trick at the finish. If he mistakenly cross-ruffs without cashing his spade winners, one of the defenders may have a chance to discard spades and later ruff one of his top spades. The general principle in cross-ruff hands is to take the winners in the side suits at the earliest opportunity.

6. *Win in either hand and stop to think!* You have no side-suit losers, so your only concern is to guard against two trump losers. The safety play is to lead to the spade king and lead low to the nine, if East follows suit. If East shows out, hop up with the ace and lead to the jack. This guards against any 4-1 trump break.

PART III

Mistakes in Defense

Mistakes in Defense

DEFENSE is the toughest part of the game. Many competent declarers commit atrocious sins the moment they become defenders.

Perhaps the chief reason is that effective defense requires the considerable mental effort of reconstructing the unseen hands. Fortunately, the defenders can make a surprising number of valid deductions from the opponents' bidding—while declarer has few such clues, and virtually none when his opponents have not entered the bidding.

On the other hand, the declarer has a considerable advantage in being able to see at a glance the total assets of his side—just by viewing his hand and dummy's. Each defender sees only *one* of his opponent's hands—the dummy—and has to figure out which of the key cards are held by his partner and which by his opponent. He can fathom many of these secrets by diligently counting out the hand—both the distribution and the high-card points.

At certain critical points, a defender can come to the correct conclusion by asking himself, "would declarer or my partner have made such and such a play if he had this card?" Ironically, one of the secrets of effective defense is giving declarer credit for pursuing a sensible line of play. Conversely, it is almost impossible to figure out what declarer is up to if he himself hasn't the foggiest notion. Against such inept declarers, the best defense is to lie back and wait for him to hand you totally unexpected tricks.

Throughout this book, however, we are assuming you are playing against competent opponents, and the plays that they make—or fail to make—give you vital data in planning your defense, provided you know what to look for.

Sometimes, as declarer, you can bring home a shaky contract without giving a moment's thought to the opponent's hand. But you will find that when you are defending a close contract, you will have to work harder in order to reconstruct the two unseen hands. That is why the greatest sin in defense is laziness, and why you will encounter fewer deadly defenders than tricky declarers.

We have already outlined some general defensive rules (page 19), but these come into play *after* you have thought out the hand and decided what suits to attack and where you expect to get your tricks.

To aid you on this inquiry, you should ask yourself certain basic questions as a matter of routine in the early stages of the defense:

1. *What do you know about the declarer's hand from the bidding?* What is his maximum and minimum point count? What distribution could he have?
2. *What do you know about partner's hand?* What do his bids—or his failure to bid—signify about his strength and distribution?
3. *What do you know about the distribution of the suit led to the first trick?* Usually, the first trick will provide clues to the strength and distribution

of that suit around the table. Once you unravel the secrets of one suit, you are well on your way to figuring out the other three.

4. *How many certain tricks does your side have?* If it appears that another trick or two is needed to set the contract, what holding could your partner possibly have that would allow you to obtain the extra needed tricks?

5. *Conversely, how many tricks seem certain for the declarer?* Can you prevent him from making the extra tricks he will need? What must your partner have to thwart declarer's plan?

With this general background, let us turn to the most common defensive mistakes.

UNIMAGINATIVE OR TAME OPENING LEADS

The fate of a hand is often decided by the opening lead. Too many players select a lead by rote, without trying to puzzle out the hand declarer has shown in the bidding and the best way to foil his likely plan. If defense is the toughest part of bridge, the opening lead is surely the most difficult aspect of defensive play. To find the "killing" lead requires imagination, flair, and technical knowledge. The best we can do here is to try to give you some guidelines.

Three elements enter into the selection of an opening lead: choice of the right card; choice of the right suit; and inferences from the bidding. Let us consider them in turn.

1. *Which card to lead.* With two or more honor cards

in sequence, it is usually right to lead the top honor in the sequence:

K Q J 2   **Q J** 2   **J** 10   **K J** 10 3 2

There are two exceptions to be noted. From a 3-card or longer holding headed by ace-king, the standard lead (for no very good reason) is the king. The lead of the ace first, followed by the king, shows a doubleton.

With two honors in sequence, the choice depends on the contract:

K Q 3 **2**   **Q J** 4 3 2

Lead the high honor in a suit contract, but fourth-best in notrump.

With a 3-card holding headed by just one honor or two honors not in sequence, the lead of the lowest card is generally right:

Q 3 **2**   **K J 2**

If four or more cards are held, lead the fourth-best (fourth from the top):

J 4 3 **2**   **K J** 4 **3** 2

There is no general agreement about what card to lead holding three or more *small* cards. Some players invariably lead the highest (**8**-7-2), but partner will have difficulty distinguishing this from the lead of a doubleton. Other players lead the lowest card (8-7-**2**), but here partner might assume the lead is from an honor.

Perhaps the best solution is to lead the middle

card, a method known as MUD. The letters stand for Middle-Up-Down, the sequence in which the cards must be played to give partner the best chance of judging the situation.

Sometimes the top card might prove valuable later on, so there is much to be said for leading the *second-best* from all weak holdings:

9 **6** 2   9 **7** 5 3   9 **7** 5 3 2

However you resolve this dilemma, make sure you so inform a new partner before beginning play.

2. *Which suit to lead.* The basic question for the opening leader to decide is whether he plans an active policy or a passive one. The general rule is:

Attack against notrump contracts but play defensively against trump contracts.

Notrump contracts are usually a race with both sides hurrying to develop their longest combined suit; the defenders can snatch an early lead if they hit the right suit at once. For example, A–Q–x–x–x is a splendid suit to lead against any notrump contract below the slam level. There is a good chance of running four tricks in the suit if partner can secure the lead and return your suit. But it is a terrible suit to open against six notrump because your aim is to make two tricks and you are likely to be leading up to declarer's king, perhaps handing him his twelfth trick. So you lead another suit and hope someone else will lead to your ace-queen.

The same suit (A–Q–x–x–x) becomes an unattractive lead against a *suit* contract. You no longer have any hope of taking four tricks in the suit, for either declarer or dummy figures to be short in the suit and will eventually be able to trump a later round.

A lead in this suit gives up a possible tenace position over declarer's king, and two potential defensive tricks may shrink to one. But if you must lead the suit, choose the ace, not a low card. This makes sure of one defensive trick; the lead of a low card may enable declarer to score his king and avoid losing any trick in the suit.

Suppose the choice of opening lead lies between these two suits:

(a) K J 5 3 2   (b) J 8 5 3 2

Suit (a) should be the lead against notrump. There is a fair chance of finding partner with the ace or queen and establishing the suit. Establishing suit (b) is a remote prospect.

But a lead from suit (b) is unlikely to give away a trick while a lead from suit (a) will probably cost a trick if the opponents hold both the ace and the queen. So lead (b) against a suit contract. Note that the risk of giving away a trick is worth taking at notrump because you may be able to run the suit, but the trump factor prevents you from taking many tricks against an opposing suit contract.

Leading away from Q–x–x or J–x–x is poor policy, as it will often give away a trick:

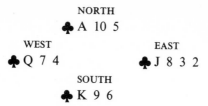

NORTH
♣ A 10 5

WEST
♣ Q 7 4

EAST
♣ J 8 3 2

SOUTH
♣ K 9 6

South makes three tricks if the defenders lead the suit, but not otherwise.

However, the risk is much less when the opener holds five or more cards in the suit:

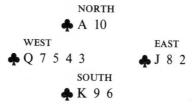

NORTH
♣ A 10

WEST
♣ Q 7 5 4 3

EAST
♣ J 8 2

SOUTH
♣ K 9 6

When the opening leader is long in the suit led, the other holdings are shorter. As dummy has only a doubleton in this case, the queen cannot be finessed and declarer can only make two tricks in the suit. (Notice that if another suit is opened and East later opens up the club suit, the jack is the winning card for the defense.)

The most productive leads against either a suit or notrump contract are from 3-card honor sequences, such as A–K–Q, K–Q–J, or even Q–J–10. These are attacking leads; at the same time, they cannot give away a trick.

Alas, such strong honor combinations are seldom available. In their absence, the safest lead against a trump contract often turns out to be a suit in which only low cards are held. This can hardly give the declarer a trick, although it may save him a guess if your partner has an honor.

All bridge rules are made to be broken. Here, too:

(a) Look for a *safe* lead against notrump:
   (1) with a very weak hand lacking entries
   (2) when the opening bidder has shown a very strong balanced hand (perhaps by opening two notrump)
   (3) when the contract is a slam

(b) Look for an *attacking* lead against a trump contract:
   (1) if dummy is likely to have a long suit which will provide discards
   (2) if you have four or more trumps (or if it seems likely that your partner has)
   (3) if the opponents have bid three suits and carefully avoided notrump. (In this last case, lead the unbid suit even from an unsafe combination such as ace-queen.)

3. *Inferences from the bidding.* "Blind leads are for deaf players" is an old bridge saying. If you do not listen to the bidding, your chance of finding the best lead is greatly reduced. Even if there is only one round of bidding, the opening leader should be able to form some rudimentary mental picture of the declarer's hand and dummy's. He will usually know something about the strength, and the distribution; with a longer bidding sequence, he may come close to a detailed picture.

This is best illustrated by some examples. In each case you sit West and have to lead against the bidding given:

SOUTH	WEST	NORTH	EAST
1 NT	Pass	Pass	Pass

You hold:

♠ Q 8 6 4   ♡ J 7   ◇ K J 7   ♣ Q 8 6 4

Lead the spade four, choosing your better major suit. You tend to lead a major suit, for the opponents are unlikely to play in notrump when they have a major-suit fit. Avoid a minor-suit lead for they may well have a concealed fit in a minor. In particular, shy away from leading clubs. Dummy may have length in clubs but could not bid the suit because a two-club response would be artificial (the Stayman Convention).

SOUTH	WEST	NORTH	EAST
1 ♡	Pass	1 NT	Pass
3 NT	Pass	Pass	Pass

You hold:

♠ 8 6 4   ♡ J 7   ◇ Q 8 6 4   ♣ K J 6 4

Lead a spade, as it is most unlikely that either opponent has four cards in that suit. (The chance that South has exactly four spades and four hearts is slight, though not out of the question; North would surely respond with one spade holding four cards in the suit.)

Unless something else looks very good, one

should generally lead the "unbid major" against notrump. If the opponents bid hearts but not spades, the chances are that they do not have spades, and vice versa.

SOUTH	WEST	NORTH	EAST
1 ♣	Pass	1 ♠	Pass
2 ♣	Pass	2 ♢	Pass
3 NT	All pass		

You hold:

♠ J 6   ♡ Q 8 5 4   ♢ 10 7 6 2   ♣ K 10 6

South's jump in notrump indicates he is well protected in the unbid suit, as he must expect a lead there. The bidding marks North with five spades and South with at least five clubs. Lead a diamond; this may well be the weak spot.

SOUTH	WEST	NORTH	EAST
1 ♢	Pass	1 ♡	Pass
1 ♠	Pass	2 ♣	Pass
2 NT	Pass	3 NT	All pass

You hold:

♠ Q 8 6   ♡ 8 7 4   ♢ K J 7 2   ♣ 10 4 3

Lead a club, since nothing else looks better. In general, dummy's second suit is a good place to attack, because one does not want to lead up to a suit bid by the declarer and the dummy's first-bid suit is probably a long one. In this particular case, North may have manufactured his club bid without a real suit; if he really had clubs he would likely have bid notrump himself at his second turn.

SOUTH	WEST	NORTH	EAST
1 ♠	Pass	1 NT	Pass
2 ♡	All pass		

You hold:

♠ K J 7 4   ♡ 10 6 2   ◇ Q 7 3   ♣ J 8 2

Lead a trump. Dummy is likely to have three trumps and a singleton or doubleton in spades. The trump lead will probably reduce declarer's prospects of ruffing spades in dummy.

SOUTH	WEST	NORTH	EAST
Pass	Pass	1 ♣	Pass
1 ◇	Pass	1 ♡	Pass
1 ♠	Pass	3 ♠	Pass
4 ♠	All pass		

You hold:

♠ 8 7   ♡ J 10 9 4   ◇ Q 10 7 6   ♣ K Q 4

When the opponents end up in the fourth suit, they will probably try to take tricks on a cross-ruff, so a trump lead is likely to be best.

It is also right to lead a trump if the bidding suggests that there will be ruffs in the dummy. But avoid this lead when holding a singleton trump, for it may trap your partner's trump honor. Moreover, partner may have four trumps and the best defense may be to keep pushing your long suit so as to wrest trump control from declarer.

OPENING LEAD QUIZ

Pick your opening lead as West, with the hand shown, after the given bidding sequence:

1. | SOUTH | NORTH |
   |-------|-------|
   | 1 ♡ | 3 ♡ |
   | 4 ♡ | Pass |

   YOU HOLD:
   ♠ A J 5 4
   ♡ 10
   ◇ J 9 8 7 6
   ♣ J 6 3

2. | SOUTH | NORTH |
   |-------|-------|
   | 1 NT | Pass |

   YOU HOLD:
   ♠ A J 3
   ♡ K 8 4 2
   ◇ 6 5
   ♣ J 9 3 2

3. | SOUTH | NORTH |
   |-------|-------|
   | 1 ♣ | 1 ♡ |
   | 1 ♠ | 3 ♠ |
   | 4 ♠ | Pass |

   YOU HOLD:
   ♠ 10 7
   ♡ J 9 7
   ◇ Q 9 5
   ♣ A Q 4 3 2

4. | SOUTH | NORTH |
   |-------|-------|
   | Pass | 1 ♠ |
   | 1 NT | Pass |

   YOU HOLD:
   ♠ 7 4
   ♡ Q J 6 4
   ◇ J 8 2
   ♣ A J 3 2

5. | SOUTH | NORTH |
   |-------|-------|
   | 1 ♡ | 1 ♠ |
   | 1 NT | Pass |

   YOU HOLD:
   ♠ A 7 5
   ♡ K 4
   ◇ J 10 8 7
   ♣ K 8 4 3

6. | SOUTH | NORTH |
   |-------|-------|
   | Pass | 1 ◇ |
   | 1 ♡ | 2 ♣ |
   | 2 ◇ | 2 ♡ |
   | Pass | |

   YOU HOLD:
   ♠ A J 10 3
   ♡ A 3 2
   ◇ 10 4
   ♣ 8 6 4 2

7. | NORTH | SOUTH |
   |-------|-------|
   | 1 NT | 3 ♡ |
   | 4 ♡ | 6 ♡ |
   | Pass | |

   YOU HOLD:
   ♠ 6 4
   ♡ J 10 4 3
   ◇ Q 5 4 2
   ♣ J 10 7 6

8. | SOUTH | NORTH |
   |-------|-------|
   | 1 ♣ | 2 ♣ |
   | 2 ♠ | 3 ♠ |
   | 4 ♠ | Pass |

   YOU HOLD:
   ♠ 9 8 4
   ♡ A K 6 2
   ◇ 7 6
   ♣ A 10 5 3

9. | SOUTH | NORTH |
   |-------|-------|
   | 2 NT | 3 NT |
   | Pass | |

   YOU HOLD:
   ♠ Q J 5
   ♡ J 8 5 3
   ◇ K 7 2
   ♣ 8 3 2

10. | SOUTH | WEST | NORTH | EAST |
    |-------|---------|-------|------|
    | 1 ♠ | 2 ♡ | 3 ♠ | 4 ♡ |
    | 4 ♠ | 5 ♣ | Dbl. | Pass |
    | 5 ♠ | All pass | | |

    YOU HOLD:
    ♠ A 8 3
    ♡ A K J 7 4
    ◇ —
    ♣ Q 9 8 5 2

ANSWERS TO OPENING LEAD QUIZ

1. *Diamond seven.* An easy one to start with. The singleton trump is almost always a bad lead, and a lead in a black suit could well give the de-

clarer a trick. A lead from five cards headed by the jack is almost completely safe, and the fourth-best seven is the orthodox choice of card.

2. *Heart two.* With no suits bid the tendency is to lead a major suit. The fourth-best heart is therefore indicated.

3. *Diamond five.* The unbid suit is usually the one to lead, and here it is important to attack diamonds before the declarer can discard diamonds on dummy's hearts. A trump is the second choice; it may stop an impending cross-ruff.

4. *Heart four.* When in doubt, lead the unbid major against notrump. The fourth-best lead is preferable to the queen, which would be correct against a trump contract.

5. *Diamond jack.* Since both majors have been bid, you want to lead a minor. The near solidity of the diamond suit earns it the preference. If the diamonds were J–6–4–2, the club suit would be a better choice.

6. *Heart two.* North has bid two suits and supported a third, so it is highly probable that he has three trumps and a singleton in the fourth suit. The trump lead should cut down the potential spade ruffs in dummy. No doubt you will want to lead the ace of trumps and a third round when you win the spade ace. (Leading the heart ace originally is inferior, as it surrenders trump control in case you want to change your defense plan.)

7. *Spade six.* Defensive prospects are excellent, because the declarer has a trump loser he does not expect. It is vital to avoid giving anything away

with the opening lead, and the spade is safest.

8. *Club ace,* with the ten to follow. Partner surely has at most one club, and we should be able to give him two ruffs to beat the contract before the declarer can win a trick. The club ten will be a suit-preference signal asking East to return a heart—the high spot asks for the higher-ranking side suit. It would be a mistake to lead the heart king first, because an opponent may have a singleton heart, and the entry for the second ruff will be lost.

9. *Spade queen.* When the declarer has a very strong balanced hand it is important not to give him any help. The spade queen will only help him if dummy produces king-ten of spades or its equivalent. Other leads are more likely to do some of declarer's work for him. The passive lead of a club would be in order against different bidding, with more strength expected in dummy. Here it may take a finesse for the declarer when he is short of entries to take it himself.

10. *Heart seven.* Prospects of making more than two tricks by normal play are poor. As partner supported hearts, there is a good chance that he has the queen, so you should try to give him the lead with that card so he can give you a diamond ruff. He will be rather surprised to win the trick, but should be able to work out that you want a ruff, and that it must be in diamonds. If the opponents are void in hearts, you have almost no chance to beat the contract anyway, and they may make an overtrick.

Now observe the experts apply these principles:

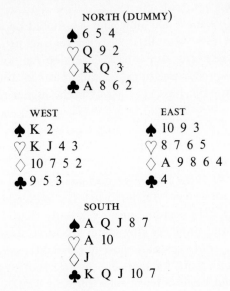

NORTH (DUMMY)
♠ 6 5 4
♡ Q 9 2
◇ K Q 3
♣ A 8 6 2

WEST
♠ K 2
♡ K J 4 3
◇ 10 7 5 2
♣ 9 5 3

EAST
♠ 10 9 3
♡ 8 7 6 5
◇ A 9 8 6 4
♣ 4

SOUTH
♠ A Q J 8 7
♡ A 10
◇ J
♣ K Q J 10 7

Neither side vulnerable.

NORTH	EAST	SOUTH	WEST
Pass	Pass	1 ♣	Pass
1 ◇	Pass	2 ♠	Pass
3 ♣	Pass	3 ♠	Pass
4 ♠	All pass		

By listening carefully to the bidding, West hit on the killing lead—the club nine. He knew that North-South held at least eight clubs between them, and if the total was more, a club ruff for East could be maneuvered.

South won in his hand and led the diamond jack, hoping to be able to discard his heart loser. West played the diamond seven—a high card in the suit the

opponents have led conventionally shows an even number of cards—and East won with the ace.

He shifted to a heart, and South had to lose four
tricks: one spade, one heart, one diamond, and one
club ruff. There was no quick entry to dummy to take
a discard on the diamonds.

It would not have helped South to play trumps immediately. West would have continued clubs, giving
his partner a ruff, and a heart return would again have
cooked declarer's goose.

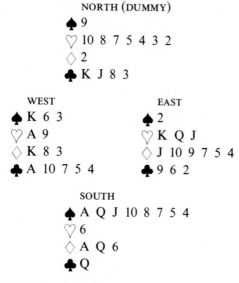

NORTH (DUMMY)
♠ 9
♡ 10 8 7 5 4 3 2
♢ 2
♣ K J 8 3

WEST
♠ K 6 3
♡ A 9
♢ K 8 3
♣ A 10 7 5 4

EAST
♠ 2
♡ K Q J
♢ J 10 9 7 5 4
♣ 9 6 2

SOUTH
♠ A Q J 10 8 7 5 4
♡ 6
♢ A Q 6
♣ Q

North-South vulnerable.

EAST	SOUTH	WEST	NORTH
Pass	1 ♠	2 ♣	Pass
Pass	4 ♠	All pass	

With a wide choice of leads, a trump would have been the most effective. Actually, West led the club ace and was faced by an unusual situation at the second trick. It was likely that South's queen of clubs was a singleton, so it was vital to keep South out of the dummy.

Shifting to a low trump would have been fatal, for the nine would have won in the dummy and South would have discarded two losers on the clubs. The winning play—a most remarkable one—was to lead the spade king. This sacrificed a trump trick but left South with three more inescapable losers.

The same sensational trump play would be essential if West had led the ace and another heart. South would have ruffed and led the club queen, forcing West to find the spade king lead to defeat the contract.

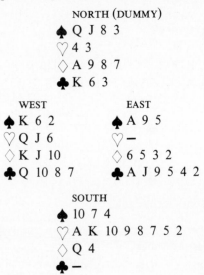

NORTH (DUMMY)
♠ Q J 8 3
♡ 4 3
◇ A 9 8 7
♣ K 6 3

WEST
♠ K 6 2
♡ Q J 6
◇ K J 10
♣ Q 10 8 7

EAST
♠ A 9 5
♡ —
◇ 6 5 3 2
♣ A J 9 5 4 2

SOUTH
♠ 10 7 4
♡ A K 10 9 8 7 5 2
◇ Q 4
♣ —

SOUTH	WEST	NORTH	EAST
4 ♡	Pass	Pass	Pass

There was some risk in leading away from either of the kings, or from the club queen. West therefore chose to lead the heart queen, which could only hurt the defense in the improbable event that East held a singleton heart king.

West's later defense did not measure up to his stellar opening lead. He noted his partner's discard of the club five on the first trick and correctly deduced East had club strength. But, alas, he saw no further.

When declarer led a spade at trick two, West rushed up with his king in order to lead the club queen. This fazed South not at all. He ruffed, cashed the heart king, and led the spade ten. This established dummy's fourth spade for a discard of declarer's losing diamond, and the contract was home.

If West had bothered to reconstruct declarer's hand, he would have placed the spade ace in his partner's hand and allowed East to win the first spade so he could lead a diamond to West's king. It was vital to set up a diamond trick before the spade suit was established for a diamond discard.

How could West know that declarer did not hold the spade ace? Well, first because declarer was unlikely to have an outside ace together with a suit of A–K–10–9–x–x–x–x and make a pre-emptive bid as dealer. The correct bid would be one heart.

Secondly, West should realize there is no hope for the defense if declarer holds the spade ace, for he knows that declarer has seven heart tricks and can see the eighth trick in dummy's diamond ace. If South has the spade ace, he can easily manufacture the two tricks he needs in spades. On that reasoning, West should place East with the spade ace, as the only hope to defeat the contract.

When this deal was replayed in a team-of-four match, West led the diamond jack. This appears to be the one normal lead that allows the contract to make, but South had no way of knowing that West had led from the king. He put up the diamond ace in dummy, expecting to make eight trump tricks, one spade, and one diamond. He did not want to risk playing low from dummy on the first trick, which might easily have led to the loss of a diamond, two spades, and a spade ruff. But the actual 3–0 trump division was a killer, and he went down one trick because he made the right play. Virtue is not always its own reward in this game.

FAILURE TO SHIFT SUITS

After the opening lead has been made and dummy's cards are exposed, each defender knows twenty-six of the cards, which is twice as much as he knew before. Each should now be able to figure out the most likely line of play to set the contract.

But it doesn't usually work out that way. Most players are inwardly insecure about their defensive play and tend to follow the straight and narrow path of "doing nothing wrong." This generally takes the form of "returning partner's suit." A major defensive fault is blindly continuing with the suit that was opened. It usually seems both safe and easy to do so. But the opening lead was made in the dark, and the appearance of dummy's cards has shed new light on the hand. It may well be that the opening lead has struck pure defensive gold; equally, it could prove to be a disaster.

Surely it is pure laziness to continue thoughtlessly with the suit first led. But how can you avoid this common mistake? How will you know when to persevere with the suit led and when to switch to another? Ask yourself these questions and you will solve such problems more often:

1. *Is it really safe to continue the same suit?* Don't be deterred by the fact that declarer will ruff the next round. Making him ruff is usually—but not invariably—to the defenders' advantage. An exception is when one defender has a long trump holding of moderate strength. Declarer may then welcome the chance to ruff, because it will help him to develop an endplay or throw-in against the defender with the trump length.

   But if you lead the king from an ace-king or king-queen combination, and win the trick, you must consider whether a continuation will give the declarer a trick. In each case, the card partner plays will usually solve the problem: He will play a high card if he wants a continuation, a low one if he does not.

   Even if dummy is about to ruff, it may be sensible to continue the suit. Perhaps ruffs in dummy are inevitable, because dummy has four or more trumps there; still, it may be right to force an immediate ruff—either to use up one of dummy's entries prematurely or to weaken declarer's control of the trump suit.

2. *Will a trump shift help?* If dummy has one to three trumps and a short side suit, a trump shift may cut down its ruffing power, but this may be difficult to judge. It may be that declarer plans to establish a side suit rather than to take ruffs in dummy. Also, you must consider whether a trump lead will expose partner's trump holding of Q–x–x, A–J–x, J–x–x–x, or something similar.

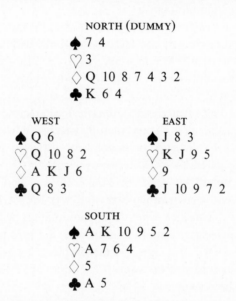

NORTH (DUMMY)
♠ 7 4
♡ 3
♢ Q 10 8 7 4 3 2
♣ K 6 4

WEST
♠ Q 6
♡ Q 10 8 2
♢ A K J 6
♣ Q 8 3

EAST
♠ J 8 3
♡ K J 9 5
♢ 9
♣ J 10 9 7 2

SOUTH
♠ A K 10 9 5 2
♡ A 7 6 4
♢ 5
♣ A 5

By bidding not fit to print, South reaches a contract of four spades. West leads the diamond king, and knows all about that suit when the king wins.

It is clear that South will be ruffing heart losers in dummy, so West must shift to a trump, even if it costs him a trump trick. And his lead must be the queen,

providing for the actual situation in which East has
J–x–x. South wins the queen with the ace or king, and
is limited to one ruff in the dummy. If he takes the
ruff, East's spade jack becomes the setting trick. And
if he uses dummy's trump to capture the spade jack
with a finesse, he remains a trick short.

3. *In notrump, do you have a chance to establish some
other suit?* After the first trick, it may be clear
that declarer has complete control of the suit first
led. In that case, the defender may have to decide whether his partner might have a suitable
holding in another suit to permit its establishment.

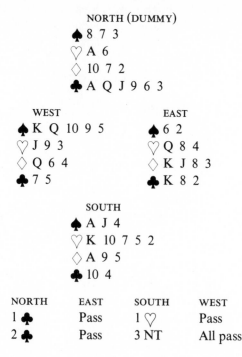

NORTH (DUMMY)
♠ 8 7 3
♡ A 6
♢ 10 7 2
♣ A Q J 9 6 3

WEST
♠ K Q 10 9 5
♡ J 9 3
♢ Q 6 4
♣ 7 5

EAST
♠ 6 2
♡ Q 8 4
♢ K J 8 3
♣ K 8 2

SOUTH
♠ A J 4
♡ K 10 7 5 2
♢ A 9 5
♣ 10 4

NORTH	EAST	SOUTH	WEST
1 ♣	Pass	1 ♡	Pass
2 ♣	Pass	3 NT	All pass

North-South bid aggressively to three notrump, which will always succeed if the club suit can be run. Even as the cards lie, the defense must be good to succeed.

West leads the spade king, and South ducks, as he must. West takes note of his partner's deuce and rightly decides that there is no future in spades. As South has bid hearts it is unlikely that the defense can break through there, so the only hope lies in diamonds.

He shifts to the diamond four, and whether South holds up or not he cannot avoid the loss of five tricks.

4. *Is passive defense indicated?* On many deals, the policy is to sit back and do nothing—at any rate, nothing that might cost a trick. If there is no indication that declarer will be able to obtain any discards or ruffs, look for a safe play.

DO YOU SHIFT QUIZ

1.

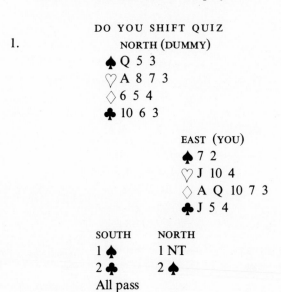

NORTH (DUMMY)
♠ Q 5 3
♡ A 8 7 3
◇ 6 5 4
♣ 10 6 3

EAST (YOU)
♠ 7 2
♡ J 10 4
◇ A Q 10 7 3
♣ J 5 4

SOUTH	NORTH
1 ♠	1 NT
2 ♣	2 ♠
All pass	

West leads the diamond two and your ace collects the king from South. What do you lead to trick two?

2.

NORTH (DUMMY)
♠ 10 7
♡ 10 6 3
◇ A J 7 4
♣ K 10 6 2

WEST (YOU)
♠ Q 8 6
♡ A K 9 5 4
◇ 6 5
♣ J 5 3

SOUTH	NORTH
1 ♠	1 NT
2 ♠	All pass

You lead the king of hearts, on which your partner, East, plays the two and South, the eight. What next?

3.

NORTH (DUMMY)
♠ 7 5
♡ A 5 4
◇ 8 3 2
♣ K Q J 9 5

WEST (YOU)
♠ 8 6 2
♡ K 10 6
◇ A J 9 5 4
♣ 10 6

SOUTH   NORTH
4 ♠   All pass

You lead the ace of diamonds, on which your partner plays the six and South, the king. Now what?

ANSWERS TO DO YOU SHIFT QUIZ

1. *Continue with a diamond*—any diamond. This is a case where you can picture declarer's distribution exactly. He surely has five spades, four clubs, one diamond, and therefore three hearts. By making him ruff diamonds, you can weaken his trumps and he may have trouble winning a trick with his fourth club, which you know will be a winner, for you can see that the suit breaks 3–3.

2. *Play the ace of hearts,* despite partner's discouraging signal. This is quite safe: if West has more than two hearts, a third round will force South to ruff, which cannot harm the defense. And if East has a singleton or doubleton heart, he will be able to ruff out South's winner. (Of course, East cannot have a small doubleton heart—for he would have played the higher card to encourage you to continue and give him a ruff—but he might have a doubleton queen.)

3. *Shift to the heart six.* Your best chance to defeat the contract is to make two hearts and the club ace, presumably in East's hand, in addition to the diamond ace. But if you play passively, declarer will no doubt be able to draw trumps and establish dummy's club suit, avoiding heart losers. So

you have to attack hearts, hoping East has the queen; if declarer has it, the chance of a successful defense is slight indeed.

Now witness some sparkling defenses:

NORTH (DUMMY)

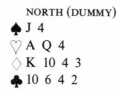

♠ J 4
♡ A Q 4
◇ K 10 4 3
♣ 10 6 4 2

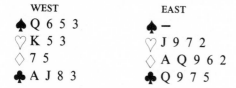

WEST	EAST
♠ Q 6 5 3	♠ —
♡ K 5 3	♡ J 9 7 2
◇ 7 5	◇ A Q 9 6 2
♣ A J 8 3	♣ Q 9 7 5

SOUTH
♠ A K 10 9 8 7 2
♡ 10 8 6
◇ J 8
♣ K

East-West vulnerable.

SOUTH	WEST	NORTH	EAST
3 ♠	Pass	Pass	Pass

West opened the diamond seven as the safest lead and East won with the queen. There was now only one way to defeat the contract, and East found it. He returned the heart deuce.

This is certainly an unusual play—"lead up to weakness" is the old whist rule—but it was completely safe. East could see that declarer had two heart tricks in any event; in the unlikely event that South held the king, the lead would cause no harm.

As it was, West had the king and played it, forcing dummy's ace. Declarer attacked trumps. When West won his spade queen, he led a second heart. This effectively prevented South from discarding a heart loser on a diamond in dummy, because dummy's two heart entries disappeared before the trumps could be drawn.

Any other lead at the second trick would enable declarer to make his contract, for he would have time to establish a diamond winner in dummy on which to discard his heart loser.

NORTH (DUMMY)
♠ —
♡ K J 7
♢ Q 10 3
♣ K J 8 6 4 3 2

WEST
♠ K J 9 5 3
♡ 10 4
♢ 8 7 6
♣ Q 7 5

EAST
♠ Q 7 4
♡ Q 9 6
♢ K J 5 4 2
♣ A 10

SOUTH
♠ A 10 8 6 2
♡ A 8 5 3 2
♢ A 9
♣ 9

SOUTH	WEST	NORTH	EAST
1 ♠	Pass	2 ♣	Pass
2 ♡	Pass	3 ♡	Pass
4 ♡	All pass		

West led the diamond eight and East's jack forced the ace. The nine of diamonds was returned, and when East won with the king, he had to make a crucial play.

He worked out—correctly up to a point—that South was aiming to discard a club on dummy's diamond queen. He therefore cashed the club ace, making sure he wouldn't lose it, and then led a spade.

This failed to ruffle declarer. He won with the ace, cashed the two high trumps—refusing the chance to finesse—and discarded two of his spade losers on the diamond queen and club king. Next, he ruffed a club, as East discarded a spade. But East still had to follow suit when declarer now ruffed a spade in dummy. By now, dummy's club suit was established, so declarer led one, on which he discarded his last spade. It did not matter whether or not East ruffed, for the master trump was the third and last trick for the defense.

East should have seen that it was vital to limit ruffs in dummy. The winning play at the third trick is a trump from his queen, deliberately sacrificing a potential trick. Declarer can win in dummy and discard his club loser on the diamond queen, but he cannot then set up the club suit. He can make nine tricks by crossruffing, but there is no tenth trick.

Two famous players—Norman Kay and Peter Leventritt—found an unusual defense on the following deal from an International Team Trial:

NORTH (DUMMY)
♠ 9
♡ 7 4 2
◇ K 9
♣ A K J 10 9 5 2

WEST
♠ 10 6 4
♡ K Q 10 8
◇ A J 5 2
♣ 7 6

EAST
♠ 8 7 2
♡ A J 5 3
◇ Q 7 6
♣ Q 8 3

SOUTH
♠ A K Q J 5 3
♡ 9 6
◇ 10 8 4 3
♣ 4

NORTH	EAST	SOUTH	WEST
1 ♣	Pass	1 ♠	Pass
2 ♣	Pass	4 ♠	All pass

The opening lead against four spades was the heart king, winning the trick. Any routine defense now permits South to make his game. Suppose, for example, that the defenders continue hearts. South ruffs the third round and draws trumps—grateful for the lucky 3–3 break. One club ruff sets up that suit, and the diamond king provides entry to play off club winners, on which declarer throws his losing diamonds.

Obviously, the diamond entry must be removed early, if the defense is to succeed. Most players in the West seat would cash a second heart and then lead the ace and another diamond. But this is not good enough. Declarer discards one diamond on the second high club, ruffs a heart to get to his hand in order to ruff a second diamond in dummy. Now he trumps a club high in his hand and draws trumps to score his game.

The winning defense effectively removes dummy's diamond entry without permitting a diamond ruff. West must lead a *low* diamond at the third trick. There is time enough to lead a trump when declarer plays a second diamond to try to set up a diamond ruff. With this sequence of plays, declarer is prevented from making a diamond ruff or running dummy's club suit.

A DISINCLINATION TO DUCK

The old whist rule says "second hand low," and this is one of the better rules of thumb. The average player is but dimly aware of the *exceptions* to this rule, and this is a classic case of "a little knowledge is dangerous."

Look in on an average game: Declarer has led from his hand (or dummy's); the next player pauses, thinks, and finally plays a card. His thought is not a complete waste: Every so often, second hand will make the correct play of an honor.

But what about the times he plays a low card after all that agony? It is a dull declarer indeed who will not realize that second hand holds an honor; this clue may be all he needs to alter his line of play and bring home a marginal contract.

Until and unless you are able to diagnose *quickly* the cases where it is right to play second-hand high, you will get better results by always playing low *quickly*. You will have to train yourself—or, rather, break an old habit in order to acquire this new one. But it is well worth the effort.

You are West, with this layout, defending a heart contract, and South leads the club deuce at an early stage in the play. How do you play?

NORTH (DUMMY)
♣ K J 7 5

WEST (YOU)
♣ A 8 6 3

SOUTH
♣ 2 led

Play low without hesitation. If declarer has the queen, your ace can wait. And if your partner has the queen, he must be given a chance to make it. Without any clues, declarer is likely to play the jack from dummy —and you will probably make two tricks in the suit.

To play the ace would solve declarer's problem for him. And to think about playing the ace is equally wrong, for the hesitation tells declarer that you have the ace and he will know to play the king from dummy.

Of course, it is improper to hesitate when you have nothing to hesitate about. Thus, the hesitation clearly reveals that you have the ace.

Even if you knew, in some way, that declarer held a singleton club, it is usually wrong to put up the ace. Although the play of the ace guarantees one trick in the suit for you, it also insures one for declarer. Left to himself, he might play dummy's jack and make no club trick at all; so you should be willing to take the slight risk of letting him escape without a club loser.

The same approach applies when the lead comes from dummy on your right: Do not put up an ace merely because dummy's singleton has been led. A prompt play of a low card nearly always works.

Here's a typical layout:

NORTH (DUMMY)
♣ 4 led

EAST (YOU)
♣ A 9 5 3

SOUTH
♣ K Q 10

If you go up with your ace on the lead of the four, declarer makes two club tricks; if you duck, he makes but one. Unless you tip him off by your hesitation, he will probably finesse the ten; then he must lose *two* club tricks before he can get his one.

Suppose the strong holding is in dummy:

NORTH (DUMMY)
♣ K Q 10

WEST (YOU)
♣ A 9 5 3

SOUTH
♣ 4 led

You duck the lead of the four, but dummy's king is played. What's more, declarer returns to his hand to lead a *second* club. Don't panic or give the show away. Instead, play low again nonchalantly. Declarer must now guess what card to play. Since few defenders possess the knowledge and discipline to play low twice with calm when holding the ace, declarer will no doubt play East for this card and will therefore finesse the ten into partner's jack.

If declarer guesses correctly and puts up the queen on the second club lead, you have the satisfaction of knowing you made life difficult for him. And, if he originally had a singleton club and *stole* a club trick, remember that your duck prevented him from making *two* club tricks, on which he could discard *two* of his losers.

To be sure, there are times when it is right to hop up with the ace:

(1) when it is the setting trick
(2) when your side can cash out enough tricks immediately to set the contract
(3) when declarer does not need discards

Case (1) is easy enough to diagnose, but (2) and (3) are tougher. Many times in case (2), your tricks won't run away, even if you duck. As for (3), you pay off— it does not happen often.

In sum, the odds are all with you if you save your aces with stoical calm.

Now, let's give the defense the king-queen.

NORTH (DUMMY)

♣ A J 9

WEST (YOU)

♣ K Q 5

SOUTH

♣ 2 led

If West is quite sure that one club trick will be enough to defeat the contract, he can of course split his honors by playing the queen. But normally the better course is to play low. You hope that your partner has the ten, and will make a trick with that card. Without any revealing hesitation from you, declarer's proper play is the nine, hoping to find you with the king-ten or queen-ten—twice as likely as your actual king-queen holding.

Let's examine these principles in a couple of full deals:

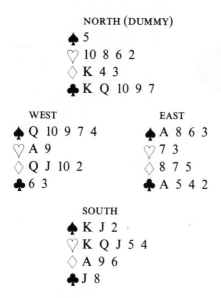

NORTH (DUMMY)
♠ 5
♡ 10 8 6 2
♢ K 4 3
♣ K Q 10 9 7

WEST
♠ Q 10 9 7 4
♡ A 9
♢ Q J 10 2
♣ 6 3

EAST
♠ A 8 6 3
♡ 7 3
♢ 8 7 5
♣ A 5 4 2

SOUTH
♠ K J 2
♡ K Q J 5 4
♢ A 9 6
♣ J 8

Against a contract of four hearts, West leads the diamond queen and South wins with the king in dummy. He leads the spade five, and the contract stands or falls on East's play: He must duck like a flash. If he puts up the ace, South will be able to discard a diamond from dummy on the spade king and ruff a diamond, limiting his losers to three aces.

And if East merely thinks about playing his ace, South will know what to do: He will put up the king confidently. Thus, the only chance for the defense is for East to play low quickly. South is then likely to play the jack from his hand, figuring that if East held the ace, he might have played it or paused before playing low.

East wins the spade queen and continues with a second diamond. Now declarer cannot escape a diamond loser, in addition to one spade, one heart, and one club, so the contract must fail.

NORTH (DUMMY)
♠ A 9
♡ A Q 4
◇ 6 4 2
♣ K Q 10 6 5

WEST
♠ Q 8 6 2
♡ 9 5
◇ Q 8 5 3
♣ A 7 3

EAST
♠ J 7 5 3
♡ K 10 7 3
◇ J 7
♣ J 9 8

SOUTH
♠ K 10 4
♡ J 8 6 2
◇ A K 10 9
♣ 4 2

The bidding:

SOUTH	WEST	NORTH	EAST
Pass	Pass	1 ♣	Pass
2 NT	Pass	3 NT	All pass

West led the spade deuce—remembering that when in doubt against a notrump contract, the lead of a major suit is preferred. South won with the king and led a low club. West ducked promptly. The queen won in dummy, and South returned to his hand with a diamond lead for a second club play. West ducked again without hesitation, and South had to guess the position of the ace and jack. He guessed wrong by playing the ten, losing to the jack, and the contract failed: Two club tricks now had to be lost and East's spade return set up two spade tricks for the defense, which West gratefully took when he won with the club ace. Declarer had only eight tricks and could not bring home a ninth in either red suit without yielding the setting trick.

What a difference if West had betrayed the club ace by hesitating. Declarer would win the first two club tricks with the king and queen, and when a third club lead dropped both the ace and jack, he would easily come to four club tricks to land his contract.

THOUGHTLESS THIRD-HAND PLAY

The old whist rule "third hand high" is right up to a point. But most players err by following it slavishly. For some strange reason, third hand seems to be in a hurry to play. But this is just the time to sit back and reflect—particularly at the first trick when you have just seen dummy and must assimilate the knowledge it provides.

Just as we have seen that second hand must play quickly, so third hand should play deliberately. The easy cases are when dummy on your right has nothing but low cards. Then you should do your best to win the trick:

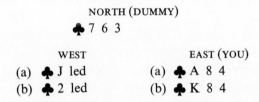

NORTH (DUMMY)

♣ 7 6 3

WEST

(a) ♣ J led

(b) ♣ 2 led

EAST (YOU)

(a) ♣ A 8 4

(b) ♣ K 8 4

In both cases, you must play your honor. Remember that the jack lead in (a) may be from K–J–10–5 or A–J–10–5—but the second is unlikely in a trump contract where it is risky to lead away from an ace.

There is one rare exception to this rule:

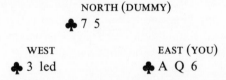

NORTH (DUMMY)

♣ 7 5

WEST

♣ 3 led

EAST (YOU)

♣ A Q 6

The contract is notrump, and you have a probable entry in another suit. It is right to play the queen rather than the ace on the opening lead. Your partner may have J–9–8–3–2, and the play of the queen will make it difficult for the declarer to hold up his king.

(For all he knows, West has the ace, and if declarer does not take his king at once, he may never get it.) Let's assume declarer does win the first trick: When you gain the lead with your side entry, you play the ace and another club to score four club tricks and set the contract.

When dummy has an honor that third player can beat, "third hand high" is usually wrong:

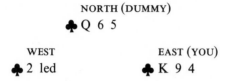

```
                NORTH (DUMMY)
               ♣ Q 6 5

     WEST                     EAST (YOU)
     ♣ 2 led                  ♣ K 9 4
```

When declarer plays low from dummy, put on the nine, whether the contract is in notrump or in a suit. You cannot gain by playing the king, but you may be preserving the king to kill the queen at a later stage. Partner could have J–10–7–2 or 10–8–7–2 in clubs.

Occasionally, this advice may lead you to abandon all hope of winning the trick:

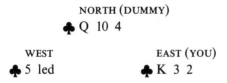

```
                NORTH (DUMMY)
               ♣ Q 10 4

     WEST                     EAST (YOU)
     ♣ 5 led                  ♣ K 3 2
```

If dummy plays low on the opening lead, so should you. If the contract is in notrump and your partner has the ace, no harm is done, for you are in a position to run the suit later. But if your partner has the jack but not the ace, you have done the right thing:

The play of the king gives the declarer three easy tricks in the suit—with a later finesse against the jack —while the duck leaves a situation where neither side can afford to lead the suit without loss.

Here is an unusual situation in which it was necessary to play "third hand low":

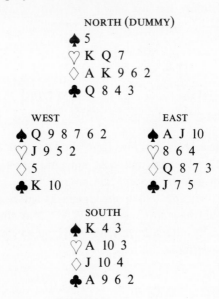

NORTH (DUMMY)
♠ 5
♡ K Q 7
♢ A K 9 6 2
♣ Q 8 4 3

WEST
♠ Q 9 8 7 6 2
♡ J 9 5 2
♢ 5
♣ K 10

EAST
♠ A J 10
♡ 8 6 4
♢ Q 8 7 3
♣ J 7 5

SOUTH
♠ K 4 3
♡ A 10 3
♢ J 10 4
♣ A 9 6 2

Both sides vulnerable.

NORTH	EAST	SOUTH	WEST
1 ♢	Pass	2 NT	Pass
3 NT	Pass	Pass	Pass

West led the spade seven and East, Peter Leventritt, made the abnormal and brilliant play of the ten. Declarer naturally assumed that West held the spade ace, and that he could not afford to let East hold the lead for a spade lead back through his king-four.

After winning the spade king at the first trick, declarer was doomed. He had to try the diamond finesse; when it lost, Leventritt played the ace and jack of spades, West overtaking to cash three more spade tricks to put declarer two down.

The normal play for East at trick one is the ace, and this was what happened when Leventritt's teammates held the North-South cards. South then held up his spade king until the third round and was able to make nine tricks despite losing the diamond finesse. East had no more spades to lead when he made his diamond trick, and West's club king was not quick enough as an entry.

The most difficult part about Leventritt's defensive play at the first trick was that it had to be made quickly. If Leventritt had thought for some time before playing the spade ten, South could have worked out what he was thinking about and countered by playing low on the ten.

Although you must disregard your partner's hesitations, it is entirely legitimate to draw inferences, at your own risk, from the hesitations of your opponents.

SLOPPY SIGNALING

Signaling is the only area in play which requires a partnership language. It is easy enough to learn the language—vastly easier than the language of bidding, for that matter—but using it appropriately requires great skill.

The expert has a great advantage over the average player: He can give signals in a routine way without great mental effort; he can read his partner's signals easily; and above all he knows when to refrain from giving signals that can only assist the declaring side.

The inexperienced player is foggy about this whole business of signaling: He doesn't understand that there are three different types of signals; he uses them incorrectly; most of the time, he doesn't bother to signal at all; he rarely knows when his partner is signaling or whether to believe him. So he makes monumental problems of simple situations.

To clear up this confusion requires, first, an understanding of the three basic types of signals:

1. *Come-on or shift.* This is the basic signal, which takes precedence over all others.

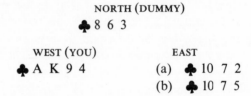

NORTH (DUMMY)
♣ 8 6 3

WEST (YOU)   EAST
♣ A K 9 4   (a) ♣ 10 7 2
                       (b) ♣ 10 7 5

Sitting West, you lead the club king against a contract of four spades. If your partner does not want a club continuation, he will play his lowest card. If he plays the two, as in (a) above, it will be a clearcut suggestion that he does not welcome a club continuation and that a shift may be indicated. If his lowest card is the five, as in (b), and the two does not appear from South, you will not be sure whether or not his partner has played the lowest available card; South may have false-carded—withholding the two in order to induce you to continue with clubs.

Conversely, if East wants his partner to continue clubs he will play *the highest card he can spare:*

WEST		EAST
♣ A K 9 4	(c)	♣ 10 3
	(d)	♣ Q 10 3

With both holdings East will drop the ten, encouraging his partner to continue with the ace and a third round. He expects to win the third round in his hand, by a ruff in (c) and by winning the queen in (d).

Sometimes the signal may be spectacular:

WEST		EAST
♣ A K 9 4	(e)	♣ Q J 8 3
	(f)	♣ Q J

In both these cases, the queen should be dropped under the king. This announces that the jack is held—unless the queen is a singleton and played perforce—and permits the opening leader to lead low to the next trick. It may be an advantage for the defense to transfer the lead from West to East.

Remember the highest-card-you-can-spare rule: A player who signals with the queen denies possession of the king and indicates that he has the jack; signaling with the jack denies the queen and suggests the ten; and so on, down the line. This applies not only in *following* suit but also in *discarding*.

Suppose East is void of spades and on a spade lead decides to discard a club from this layout:

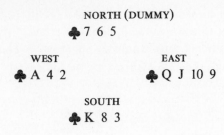

NORTH (DUMMY)

♣ 7 6 5

WEST

♣ A 4 2

EAST

♣ Q J 10 9

SOUTH

♣ K 8 3

He should play the queen, the highest club he can spare. This tells his partner that South has the king. West will therefore leave the suit strictly alone: He will know that a club lead from his side will present the declarer with a trick. Strangely, yet logically, an *encouraging* signal warns West away from a losing lead in the suit.

If East had discarded the *king,* West would lead the suit without hesitation, expecting his partner to have the queen and the jack.

What would it mean if, on a spade lead, East discarded the *jack* of clubs? It might be from either of these holdings:

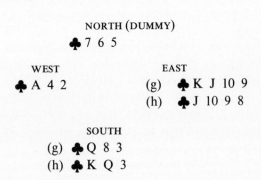

NORTH (DUMMY)

♣ 7 6 5

WEST

♣ A 4 2

EAST

(g) ♣ K J 10 9

(h) ♣ J 10 9 8

SOUTH

(g) ♣ Q 8 3

(h) ♣ K Q 3

In either case, West would know that South held the queen, but he would not know the location of the king. Playing the ace would cost a trick in either case, so it is better for West to lead low, preserving the ace to kill an honor in the South hand at a later stage.

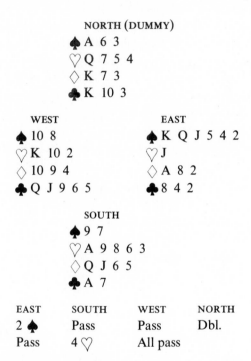

NORTH (DUMMY)
♠ A 6 3
♡ Q 7 5 4
♢ K 7 3
♣ K 10 3

WEST
♠ 10 8
♡ K 10 2
♢ 10 9 4
♣ Q J 9 6 5

EAST
♠ K Q J 5 4 2
♡ J
♢ A 8 2
♣ 8 4 2

SOUTH
♠ 9 7
♡ A 9 8 6 3
♢ Q J 6 5
♣ A 7

EAST	SOUTH	WEST	NORTH
2 ♠	Pass	Pass	Dbl.
Pass	4 ♡	All pass	

Neither side vulnerable.

South played in four hearts after East had opened with two spades—the weak two-bid used by most tournament players to show a strong 6-card suit and less strength than that of an opening bid.

West opened the spade ten and South ducked to

cut the defenders' communications. He won the spade continuation with dummy's ace, led a heart to his ace, and continued with a second heart. West won with the king and shifted to a diamond, allowing his partner to win and lead a third round of spades. This promoted West's heart ten as the setting trick.

How did West know to shift to diamonds and not clubs? Because on the second heart lead East dropped the diamond eight, an unnecessarily high card requesting a lead of that suit. He could have given the same message, indirectly and less effectively, by throwing the club two, indicating a lack of interest in clubs.

2. *Suit preference.* Sometimes you can signal when you have a choice of spot cards and there is no question of encouragement or discouragement.

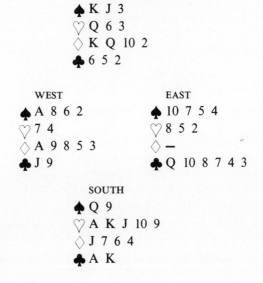

```
                    NORTH (DUMMY)
                    ♠ K J 3
                    ♡ Q 6 3
                    ◇ K Q 10 2
                    ♣ 6 5 2

        WEST                      EAST
        ♠ A 8 6 2                 ♠ 10 7 5 4
        ♡ 7 4                     ♡ 8 5 2
        ◇ A 9 8 5 3               ◇ —
        ♣ J 9                     ♣ Q 10 8 7 4 3

                    SOUTH
                    ♠ Q 9
                    ♡ A K J 10 9
                    ◇ J 7 6 4
                    ♣ A K
```

Against South's four-heart contract, West has no obvious lead. He selects the diamond ace, and is delighted with his choice when his partner discards the club three.

West now knows that the contract can be defeated. He can lead a second diamond for his partner to ruff, and regain the lead with the spade ace for a second ruff. But he also knows that his partner may go astray by failing to return a spade. The suit preference signal solves the problem:

A high card asks for a high-ranking suit, and a low card asks for a low-ranking suit.

It is assumed, with good reason, that a trump return cannot be considered. So in this case, West's second play should be the diamond nine: He plays his highest-available spot card to ask for the higher-ranking side suit, spades. If he wanted his partner to return a club, he would have led the diamond three, his lowest card, at the second trick.

The suit preference signal may be applied in a wide variety of situations, but only when it is obvious that the normal come-on or shift signal cannot be intended.

3. *The length signal.* The average player either does not know this signal or forgets to use it. When declarer leads toward dummy's long suit, the second player can give his partner a count on his length in the suit by following this rule:

Play high with an even number of cards, low with an odd number.

For example:

NORTH (DUMMY)

♣ K Q J 5 3

WEST   EAST

♣ 10 6 2   ♣ A 9 4

SOUTH

♣ 8 7

South leads the club seven to dummy's jack, West follows with the two, and East ducks. East knows that his partner must have an odd number of cards—one or three. He disregards the possibility that West has a singleton—for that would give South four clubs and East cannot duck often enough to exhaust South of clubs. So he places West with three clubs and he wins the second club lead with his ace. His aim is to play his ace on South's last card in the suit. If dummy has no side entry, declarer will not be able to win more than one club; even if dummy has an entry, East's play forces him to use it just to reach the club suit. This might make his life difficult.

If West had held a doubleton he would have played his higher card on the first lead. In a notrump contract, East would hold up until the third round of the suit, saving his ace for South's last card. But in a trump contract, East would have to consider whether to hold up twice or to win the second round in order to give partner a third-round ruff.

The length signal is useful even when your opponent holds the ace of the key suit:

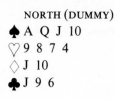

NORTH (DUMMY)
♠ A Q J 10
♡ 9 8 7 4
♢ J 10
♣ J 9 6

WEST
♠ 6 4
♡ Q J 6 2
♢ 9 8 6 3
♣ K 7 5

EAST
♠ K 9 8 5 2
♡ K 5
♢ A Q 2
♣ 8 4 3

SOUTH
♠ 7 3
♡ A 10 3
♢ K 7 5 4
♣ A Q 10 2

North-South vulnerable.

SOUTH	WEST	NORTH	EAST
1 ♣	Pass	1 ♠	Pass
1 NT	All pass		

West led the heart two, East played the king, and South won with the ace. He led the spade seven and West followed with the six, playing high with an even number of cards. The queen was played from dummy and East played low without hesitation. By ducking, he cut South's communications with dummy and left the declarer in doubt about the position of the spade king. If West had played the spade three, East would have placed South with a singleton and won the first trick.

The club nine was led from dummy for a finesse, and West won with the king. He shifted to a low diamond, and East made the good play of the queen rather than the ace. South could have cashed seven tricks at this point, but this was a duplicate game and overtricks were important. He fell into the trap of winning the diamond king and taking another finesse in spades. When the smoke had cleared he was down one: The defense made three diamond tricks, two hearts, and the two black kings.

4. *Refraining from signaling.* Learning the meaning of these basic signals is the first stage. Remembering to apply them and to watch for partner's signals is the second stage. The third stage, and just as important as the first two, is to discriminate in the use of these signals, for they inform declarer as well as partner.

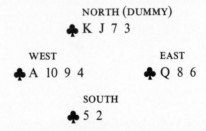

NORTH (DUMMY)

♣ K J 7 3

WEST   EAST

♣ A 10 9 4   ♣ Q 8 6

SOUTH

♣ 5 2

Let's assume that no one has played clubs, and midway in the play West has an opportunity to make a discard. A poor player will happily discard the club ten in order to advise his partner that he possesses the ace. This will be gratifying to South, because he will know what to do when he eventually leads the suit toward dummy. And it will only irritate East, who can make no use of the information and very probably knew the position of the ace without being told.

A defender should signal only when the information will help his partner and will not help the declarer— a dictum easier to state than to apply.

If the East and West cards were reversed in the above diagram, it would be equally foolish for East to signal possession of the ace. At a slightly higher level the signal might be a double-cross by a player holding the queen. Higher still it could be a triple-cross. Experts would simply play low automatically from both sides, because they would be unwilling to give the declarer even a psychological clue.

Be equally cautious when giving length signals:

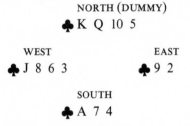

NORTH (DUMMY)
♣ K Q 10 5

WEST
♣ J 8 6 3

EAST
♣ 9 2

SOUTH
♣ A 7 4

In this position, a beginner will fare better than one who has just learned to signal. South leads low from his hand and West dutifully signals with the eight to show an even number of cards. Dummy wins with the queen and East helps declarer along by dropping the nine.

As declarer reenters his hand with the ace, both defenders happily complete their signals by playing low cards. Now, when West follows suit on the third round, South gratefully finesses the ten relying on West's signal that he started with an even number of cards in the suit. Once in a blue moon the defenders will cross up declarer by diabolically mis-signaling with 3-card holdings, but most of the time, the defensive signals are honest and guide declarer to the winning play.

By and large, you will do better by keeping your partner informed than by trying to deceive declarer. Once partner is convinced he can rely on your signaling, he may be inspired to come up with killing defenses that you did not dream possible. If you err in a situation where the information is more useful to declarer than partner, all is not lost. Declarer may not share your partner's trust, and still find a way to go wrong.

Some expert partnerships extend the length signal to all side suits* and give it precedence over the come-on signal on any trick led by the opposition. They feel that once one defender knows his partner's length in a suit, he can puzzle out the location of the high cards in that suit by the bidding and the play thus far. Try this system with your favorite partner for a session; you may be amazed how well it works and the gamut of imaginative defensive plays it opens up.

---

*In the trump suit, the signaling pattern is reversed: You play high-low to show an *odd* number of cards and up the line to indicate an even number. Most players use the trump high-low signal to indicate also the capability to ruff some side suit; a minority signal just to inform their partners, even when no ruff is possible.

PART IV

Mistakes in Behavior

Mistakes in Behavior

BRIDGE is basically played for pleasure, but the pleasure becomes annoyance when just one player is ill-mannered or unethical. Almost everyone suffers from lapses in manners or ethics from time to time. You may be an exception, but you should at least be able to recognize the behavioral errors that you may encounter in others. The following persons are all guilty of bridge misdemeanors in varying degrees:

1. The player whose tone of voice reflects his thinking. It is natural—but unethical—to bid in loud, optimistic tones with a sound hand, or in gloomy, pessimistic tones with a relatively bad hand. If your partner's inflections are revealing, you must be careful to ignore any inferences that can be drawn.

2. The player who hesitates when he has an automatic bid or play. If his mind wanders, and he suddenly finds he should have passed or followed suit while brooding on the last hand or some outside problem, he should apologize to the opponents, something like: "I'm sorry, I didn't realize it was my turn. I have nothing to think about." This will sometimes give his opponents a technical advantage, but it is better to have a bad result than a bad reputation.

3. The player who takes advantage of his partner's legitimate hesitation. An ethical player will do his best to ignore the hesitation, and in doubtful cases will take the action contrary to that suggested by the hesitation. (But it is quite proper to take advantage of an *opponent's* hesitation.)

4. The player who makes comments on the bidding and play during the progress of the deal. It is quite wrong to criticize partner's bidding after he has put down his dummy, or to state that the contract will or will not be made. A good rule is to refrain from all conversation, other than that strictly required by the game, from the time the cards are picked up until the deal is over.

5. The player who shows obvious signs of pleasure or displeasure when his partner makes a bid or play. This is one of the commonest ways in which a player may give unauthorized information to his partner.

6. The player who varies his bidding terminology and thereby tips off his partner. The proper language is strictly limited: "pass," not "I pass" or any other variation ("no bid" is acceptable if used consistently); "one club," not "a club" or just "club"; "double," not "I double" or "I double one spade."

7. The player who grumbles when he loses, or when he has to pay a penalty prescribed by the laws. (In a private game it is wise to keep handy a copy of *The Laws of Contract Bridge,* available in several editions. Use it to settle all disputes, and make it a habit to enforce all penalties.)

8. The player who calls his partner's attention to the score, or to the number of tricks needed by his side. (But in duplicate play, a player is entitled to tell his partner that he has misplaced a trick.)

9. The player who repeatedly asks for a review of the bidding or to see the previous trick. His inattention is a distraction and an irritation to the other players.

10. The player who regularly has to be reminded that it is his turn to bid or play.

11. The player who holds his cards so that his opponents can readily see them. His ethical opponents will be made uncomfortable in their attempts to keep looking away.

12. The player who gazes at an opponent who is thinking, or who watches the place from which a card is drawn in a hand. (Drawing inferences from where a card is pulled is cheating, just as much as manipulating the deal, deliberately revoking, peeking at the opponents' cards, or employing private signals.)

13. The player who, as dummy, asks to see declarer's or defenders' cards.

14. The player who is rude to his partner, or criticizes him at length. The over-critical player is often trying to cover up his own lapses. If an important technical point comes up which needs discussion, it is better to make a note to talk about it after the game is over.

15. The player who tries to teach his opponents. Even if he is by far the best player at the table, he should not give advice unasked. If his opinion is

sought, he can be non-committal or helpful, but in any event, brief and tactful.

Finally, there are a few pests who turn up only in tournament play:

16. The player who unnecessarily holds up the game for others. This may result from: having a post-mortem between deals, instead of after the second deal; failing to ask for a "late play"—a postponement of the play of a deal—when a full deal behind the field; leaving the playing area between rounds. He should wait to excuse himself when he is dummy on the second deal of a round.

17. The player who looks at an opponent's cards without permission after the deal, or still worse, takes out two hands from a board and confuses them.

18. The player who circulates rumors about the ethics of others. If he thinks his opponents have gained an unfair advantage in some way, the accepted recourse is to call the tournament director or speak to an official later in private. Rumor-mongering in bridge can be slanderous.

That concludes my Gilbertian list of the "irritating people who never would be missed."

What should you do if you meet such people? There is no easy answer.

You can give up playing with them; you can suffer in silence; you can point out the misdemeanor, if you are one of the courageous characters who reveals bad breath to close friends; or you can buy them a copy of this book and hope they read this section.

In any event, you can make sure that your own behavior is beyond reproach. This will surely make the game more enjoyable for your partner and your opponents, and with luck they will profit from your example. Then all will obtain maximum enjoyment from a great game.

GLOSSARY

Auction. The period of the bidding, concluded by three consecutive passes.

Avoidance. A play aimed at preventing a particular defender from securing the lead and making a play which will hurt the declarer.

Balancing. An action at a low level when a pass would end the bidding.

Bid. An offer on behalf of a partnership to take a certain number of tricks—the number bid plus six. Thus two spades means eight tricks with spades as trump; six notrump means twelve tricks without a trump suit.

Blackwood. An artificial convention in general use. A bid of four notrump asks partner to reveal how many aces he has. (See pages 15 and 48.)

Blank. Another term for a void, or a suit without cards in a player's hand. Also used to show that an honor card is unguarded: "a blank king" is a singleton.

Block. A situation in which entry problems in a suit make it difficult or impossible to cash potential tricks. For example, a singleton ace opposite K-x would block play of the king.

Board. The metal tray used in duplicate games to preserve the hand as dealt; hence, a duplicate deal. Also, a colloquial term for the dummy.

Bonus. Extra points awarded for: (1) bidding and making a slam; (2) making a doubled contract; (3) in rubber bridge, making a rubber; (4) in rubber bridge, holding four or five trump honors, or all the aces in notrump, in one hand; (5) in duplicate, bidding and making a game or a part score.

Break. The way in which the opponents' cards are divided in a particular suit.

Call. A pass, bid, double, or redouble during the auction.

Cash. To play a card which is sure to win a trick.

Claim. A demand for obvious tricks, made by exposing one's remaining cards.

Closed hand. The declarer's cards.

Come-on. The play of an unnecessarily high card in defense as a signal to encourage a continuation of the suit by partner.

The subsequent play of the concealed low card may complete the signal.

Competitive. An auction in which both sides take part actively. Also, a bid made in the hope of pushing the opponents to a higher level.

Concede. To surrender obvious losing tricks toward the end of a deal.

Contract. The final bid, which determines the trump suit and the number of tricks being attempted.

Control. Ability to win the first or second trick in a suit. In a suit contract, an ace or a void is a first-round control, a king or a singleton is a second-round control.

Convention. An agreement between partners that a particular bid shall have a specialized meaning. This must be made known to the opponents.

Cover. In second position, to play a high card higher than the one led. The card led must be a significant one, usually an honor.

Cross-ruff. A play procedure in which the declarer makes his trumps separately by ruffing in turn in his own hand and the dummy.

Cue bid. A bid in a suit, usually the opponents' suit, which clearly cannot be a possible final contract. At a low level it shows a desire to reach game; at a high level it shows control of the suit bid and slam ambitions.

Cutting. Drawing cards to determine partnerships; or removing a block of cards from the top of the deck which the dealer will place at the bottom of the deck before he deals.

Deal. To distribute the cards in clockwise rotation, starting to the dealer's left. Also, the cards as thus distributed.

Declarer. The player who first bids for his side the suit that becomes the final contract. He conducts the play of his own hand and the dummy in combination.

Defender. One of the declarer's opponents, each responsible for the play of his own hand.

Delayed raise. Forward-going support for partner's suit, given belatedly. (Do not confuse with **preference,** which is weak.)

Discard. A play of a card in a suit that is not trump made by a player who cannot follow to the suit led. A discard cannot win a trick.

Distribution. The manner in which the cards are divided:

either the length of suits in one player's hand, or the dispersion of a suit around the table.

DOPI. A method of countering an interference bid following Blackwood: double with zero aces, pass with one, double with two, etc. (DOPE—Double odd, pass even—is the reverse treatment.)

Double. A call that roughly doubles the points at stake on a deal if followed by three passes. A double often is a conventional request to partner to name his best suit.

Doubleton. A suit in which exactly two cards are held.

Duck. Concession of a cheap trick to the opponents by a player who could win, or attempt to win, the trick if he so desired.

Dummy. The declarer's partner, who takes no part in the play. Also, his cards, which are exposed after the opening lead.

Dummy-play. The play by the declarer of his own hand and the dummy.

Duplicate. Tournament play, and the method used in tournaments which permits each deal to be played more than once.

Endplay. A maneuver which operates during the last few tricks of a deal. See **throw-in.**

Entry. A card which allows a particular hand to gain the lead.

Establish. To play a suit until one or more cards in it have become sure winners.

Exit. To get rid of the lead safely. Also, a card by which this can be done.

False-card. An unusual play of a card made with the intention of deceiving an opponent.

Finesse. An attempt to develop one or more tricks by taking advantage of the favorable position of an opposing card or cards.

Fit. The extent to which the partnership hands mesh in the selection of a trump suit. Eight cards or more of one suit in the combined hands is a "good fit."

Five-card majors. A popular convention which bars an opening bid of one spade or one heart unless five or more cards are held in the suit.

Follow suit. To play a card of the suit first led—by implication, a losing card.

Forcing. A description of a bid which a partner should not pass unless there is a positive bid to his right. Some bids are forcing for one round of bidding only, while others are forcing on both members of the partnership until game is reached.

Forcing two. An alternative term for **strong two,** which see.

Fourth-highest (or **fourth-best**). The general practice of leading the fourth-best card from a suit of four or more cards.

Fourth-suit forcing. The theory that if four different suits are bid by one side in the first two rounds of bidding, the fourth bid promises no strength in the suit.

Freak. A hand of thirteen cards with wild distribution, such as one containing eight or more cards in a suit.

Game. A contract which, if made, scores 100 points or more. Usually three notrump, four spades or hearts, five clubs or diamonds, but less for a side that owns a part score.

Grand slam. A bid for all thirteen tricks, earning a large bonus if successful.

Hand. A particular deal of 52 cards. Also, the cards held by one player.

High-low. See **come-on.**

Hold up. To postpone the winning of a sure trick in a suit in which the opponents have strength.

Honor. An ace, king, queen, jack, or ten.

IMPs. International match points, a sliding scale type of scoring used in major team events.

Jump. Any bid which could be made in the same suit at a lower level.

Knockout. A team event in which head-to-head matches are played and defeat means elimination.

Lead. The first play to a trick.

Line. The division on a rubber bridge score between points scored toward game, written below the line, and bonus points and overtricks which go above the line.

Loser-on-loser. Playing a card which represents a sure losing trick on a losing trick in another suit.

Losers. Cards which represent potential losing tricks. This term is used in estimating the prospects both during the bidding and the play.

Major. Spades or hearts, in which a ten-trick game is possible.

Marked finesse. A finessing play which is certain to win, because the position of the crucial card has been indicated by the bidding or play.

Match-point. The unit of scoring in regular duplicate games: a pair receives one match-point for each pair with a lower score on a deal.

Minor. Diamonds or clubs, which require eleven tricks for game.

Misfit. A hand in which each player has length opposite a short suit, and therefore no good trump suit is available.

No bid. Equivalent to a pass.

Notrump. A contract without a trump suit, ranking above the four suits in the bidding.

Not vulnerable. The state of not having a game: penalties are lighter, but slam bonuses are smaller.

Overbid. A bid not justified by the strength of the bidder's hand.

Overcall. The first positive bid (other than a double or a pass) by the side that does not open the bidding.

Over-ruff. To trump higher than the right-hand opponent after a plain-suit lead.

Overtake. To play just higher than partner's card, using two high cards apparently unnecessarily in order to put the lead into the desired hand.

Overtrick. A trick made after the contract has been fulfilled, earning a small bonus.

Part score. A contract of less than game. Two part-scores usually add up to a game, provided an opposing game does not intervene.

Pass. A call which indicates that a player does not choose to make a positive bid.

Pass-out position. The position of a player who can end the auction if he chooses to pass.

Penalty. The score received by the defending side when a contract fails.

Penalty double. A double made with the expectation of defeating the opponents' contract.

Percentage play. The play indicated by mathematical analysis of particular situations in the play of the dummy.

Phantom save. A sacrifice bid made when the opposing contract would not have succeeded.

Pivot game. A game of rubber bridge in which each player partners the other three in turn.

Plain suit. See **side suit.**

Point count. The standard method of valuing the strength of a hand: ace = 4; king = 3; queen = 2; jack = 1.

Post-mortem. A discussion of the bidding and play after the hand is over.

Pre-emptive. A high-level bid usually skipping two or more levels, showing a long suit with little outside strength.

Preference. A bid which returns to partner's first-bid suit.

Raise. A bid in a suit just bid by partner.

Rebid. Any bid by a player who has previously made a positive bid.

Redouble. A bid which further increases the points at stake when an opponent has doubled a contract bid by the redoubler's side.

Response. A bid in reply to partner's bid, usually to the opening bid.

Reverse. A strength-showing bid of a second suit, usually at the level of two, which makes it impossible for partner to return to the original suit at the same level.

Revoke. A failure to follow suit when able to do so, a breach of the laws usually subject to a two-trick penalty.

Rubber. In the basic form of bridge for four players, a series of deals constituting a unit. The rubber is concluded when one side scores two games, and at that point scores are added and partnerships may change.

Ruff. To trump a trick. Also, the act of trumping.

Ruff-and-discard. A play, usually unwise, which permits the opponents to trump in either hand. Also called "ruff-and-sluff."

Run. To lead a series of winning cards in one suit. Also, to escape into a possibly better contract when your side has been doubled for penalties.

Sacrifice. A bid made defensively with no hope of success, on the theory that the penalty would give the opponents fewer points than they would score by making their own contract.

Safety play. A play of a single suit aimed at guarding against a bad division in the interests of making the contract, perhaps giving up a possible overtrick in the process.

Save. The same as **sacrifice,** which see.

Sequence. Cards touching in rank, such as Q-J-10.

Set. To defeat the contract.

Shuffle. To mix the cards together in preparation for the subsequent deal.

Side entry. An honor card which permits a hand with a long, strong suit to gain the lead and make tricks.

Side suit. A suit other than the trump suit. Also "plain suit."

Signal. A legal message transmitted by one defender, through his choice of cards, to guide the play of the other.

Singleton. A card held by a player who has no others in that suit.

Skip bid. Any bid which could have been made legally at a lower level.

Slam. A bid of six or seven, earning a large bonus if successful. The small slam, for twelve tricks, is worth 500 or 750 points according to vulnerability; the grand slam, a rare contract, is worth 1000 or 1500 points.

Sluff. Colloquial term for **discard.**

S.O.S. redouble. A redouble made by a player whose side has been doubled for penalties. It is an instruction to partner to look for a better contract.

Splitting honors. The second-hand play of an honor by a player with two touching honors (usually king-queen or queen-jack) when a small card could be played.

Spot cards. All cards lower than the jack.

Squeeze. A play which gains one trick, sometimes more, by forcing an opponent to discard disadvantageously when he must try to guard more than one suit.

Stayman. A widely played convention in which a response of two clubs to an opening notrump bid asks the opener to show a major suit. (See page 16.)

Stopper. An honor holding which is certain or likely to prevent the opponents from making a series of tricks in one suit at notrump.

Strong two. The traditional bidding style in which all opening two-bids in a suit guarantee the strength needed for a game contract. This has been virtually abandoned in expert play.

Suit preference. A method of signaling in defense. (See page 198.)

Takeout double. A double of a low-suit bid which asks partner to select an unbid suit. The converse is **penalty double**.

Team of four. A duplicate contest between two or more teams, in which four players compete at any one time. A team may consist of five or six players.

Tempo. A trick viewed as a time unit when the play has the characteristics of a race. The side that is ahead in the race "has the tempo." Also, the speed at which cards are played.

Tenace. A holding of two honors not quite in sequence—ace-queen, king-jack, or queen-ten.

Throw-in. A play, normally in the later stages of a deal, which forces a defender to win and make a losing lead—either by giving a ruff-and-discard (in a suit contract) or by leading a suit to declarer's advantage.

Trick. Four cards played in clockwise rotation, won by the highest card in the suit led unless a trump is played.

Trump. A card of the suit named in the final contract. It will win any trick unless a higher trump is played. Also, to play such a card when void in the side suit led.

Unblocking. Play of an unnecessarily high card, apparently wastefully, so that the hand opposite can win a subsequent trick in the same suit.

Underbid. A bid which suggests less strength than the bidder actually has.

Underlead. A lead of a low card when a higher card is held.

Undertrick. Each trick by which the declarer falls short of his contract, resulting in a penalty.

Void. A suit in which a player has no cards.

Vulnerable. The situation of having a game, which increases penalties but also slam bonuses.

Weak jump overcall. Pre-emptive use of the jump overcall (two spades over one heart, for instance). Roughly equivalent to a **weak two**.

Weak two. An opening bid of two spades, hearts, or diamonds used pre-emptively to show a strong six-card suit and little else.

Winners. Cards that are sure to make tricks, either because they are high cards or because of length in a suit.

Yarborough. A worthless hand, lacking an honor card.